THE WILL OF DARTH VADER

Script **Tom Taylor**

Pencils **Brian Koschak**

Inks **Dan Parsons**

Colors **Michael Wiggam**

Lettering **Michael Heisler**

Cover art **Sean McNally**

Dark Horse Books®

THIS STORY TAKES PLACE APPROXIMATELY THREE YEARS AFTER THE BATTLE OF YAVIN.

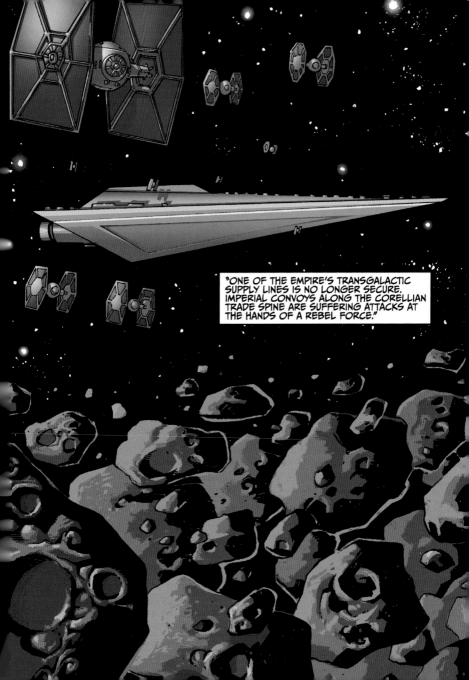

"ONE OF THE EMPIRE'S TRANSGALACTIC SUPPLY LINES IS NO LONGER SECURE. IMPERIAL CONVOYS ALONG THE CORELLIAN TRADE SPINE ARE SUFFERING ATTACKS AT THE HANDS OF A REBEL FORCE."

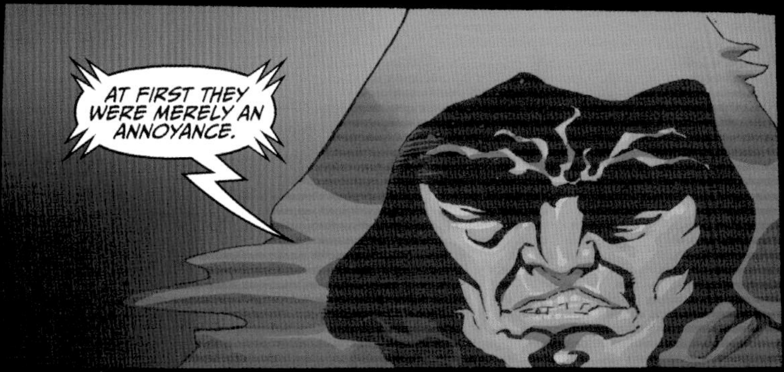
AT FIRST THEY WERE MERELY AN ANNOYANCE.

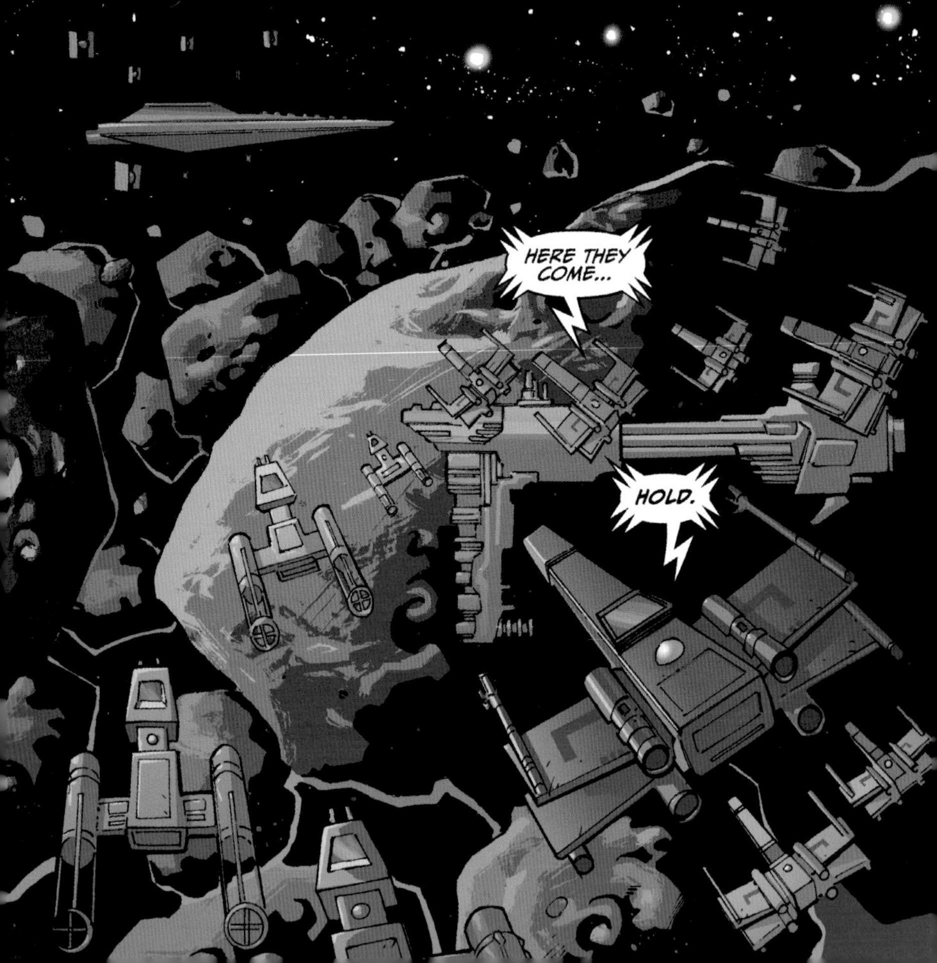
HERE THEY COME...
HOLD.

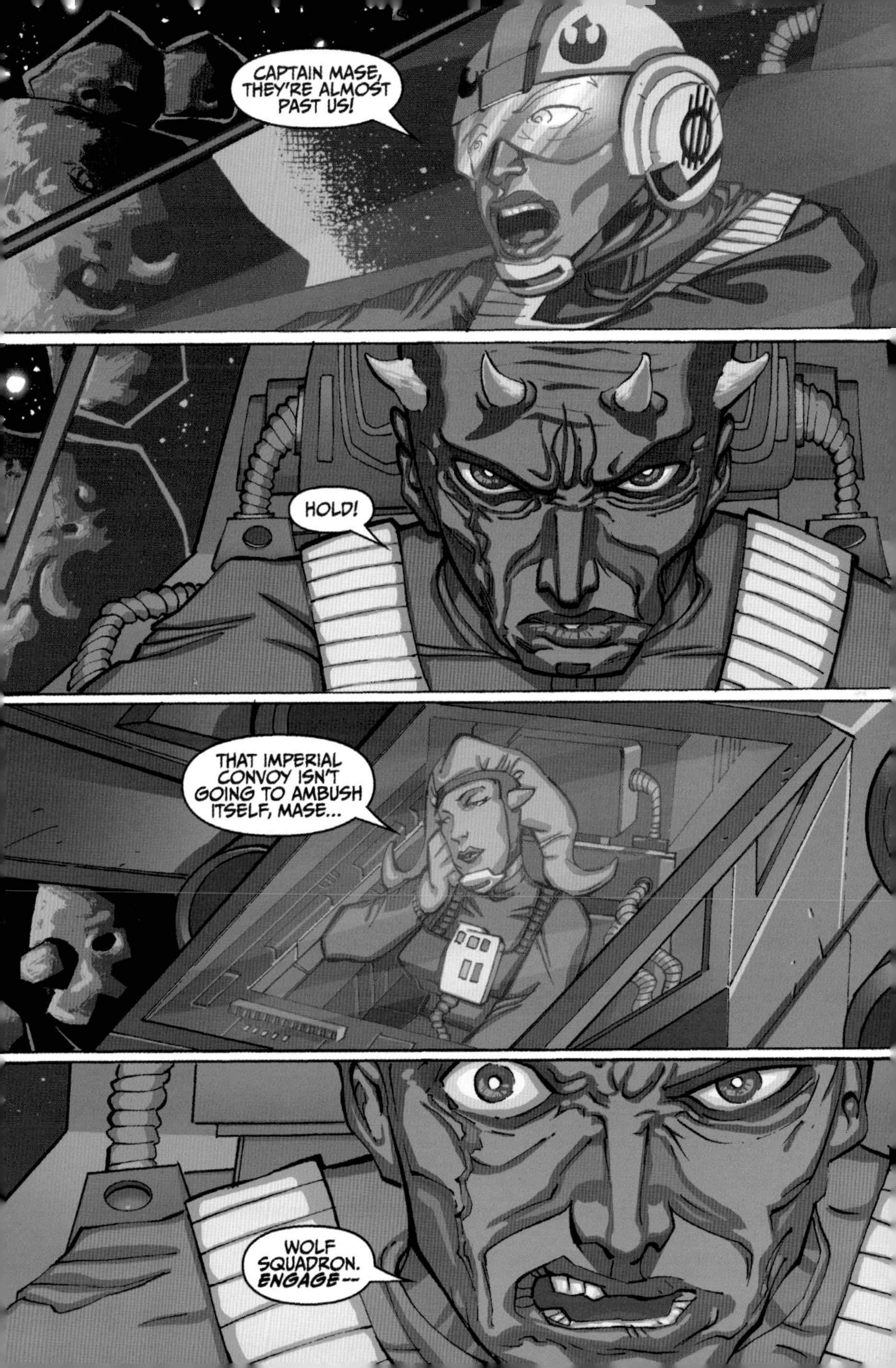
CAPTAIN MASE, THEY'RE ALMOST PAST US!
HOLD!
THAT IMPERIAL CONVOY ISN'T GOING TO AMBUSH ITSELF, MASE...
WOLF SQUADRON. *ENGAGE--*

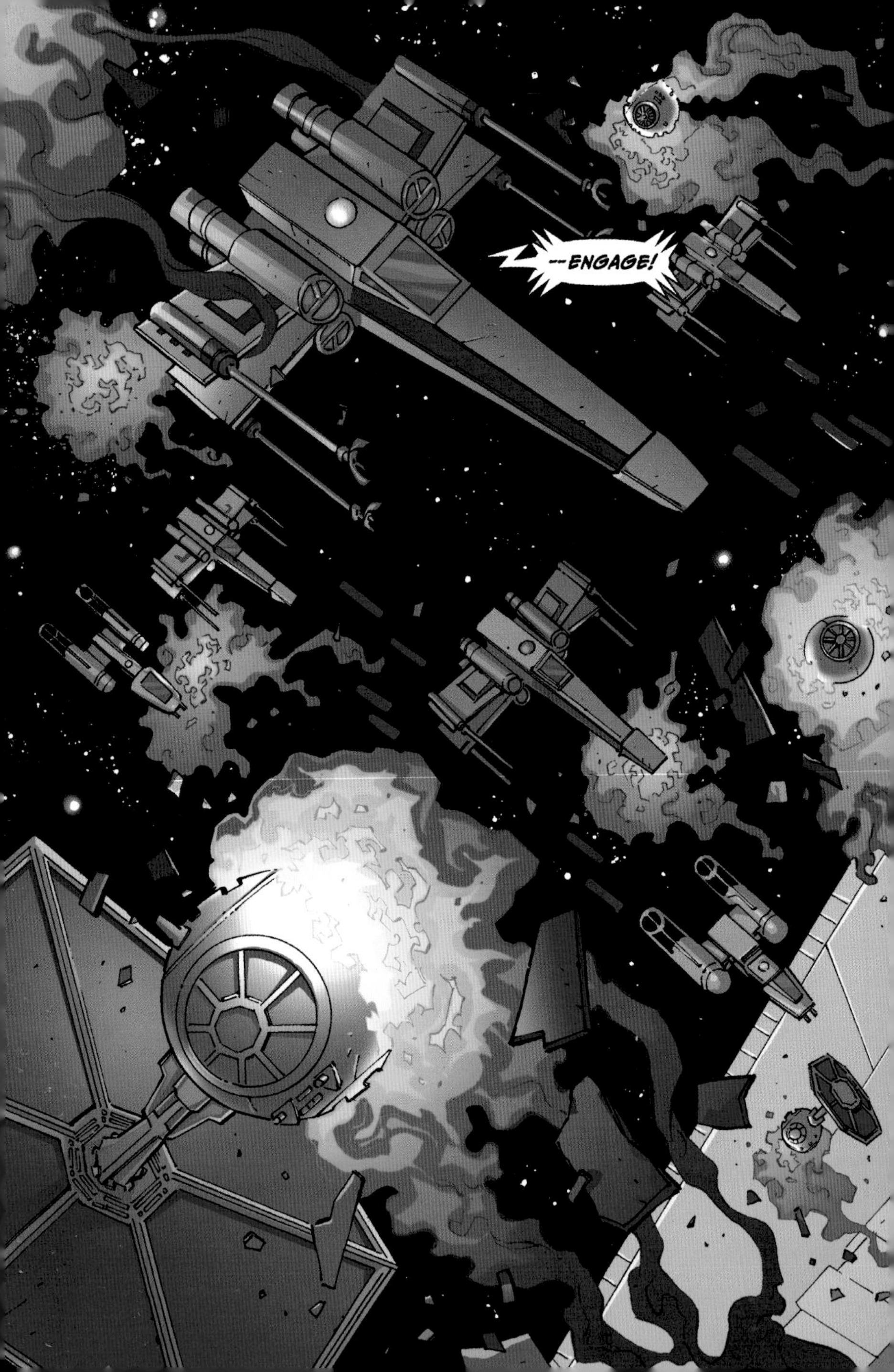
--ENGAGE!

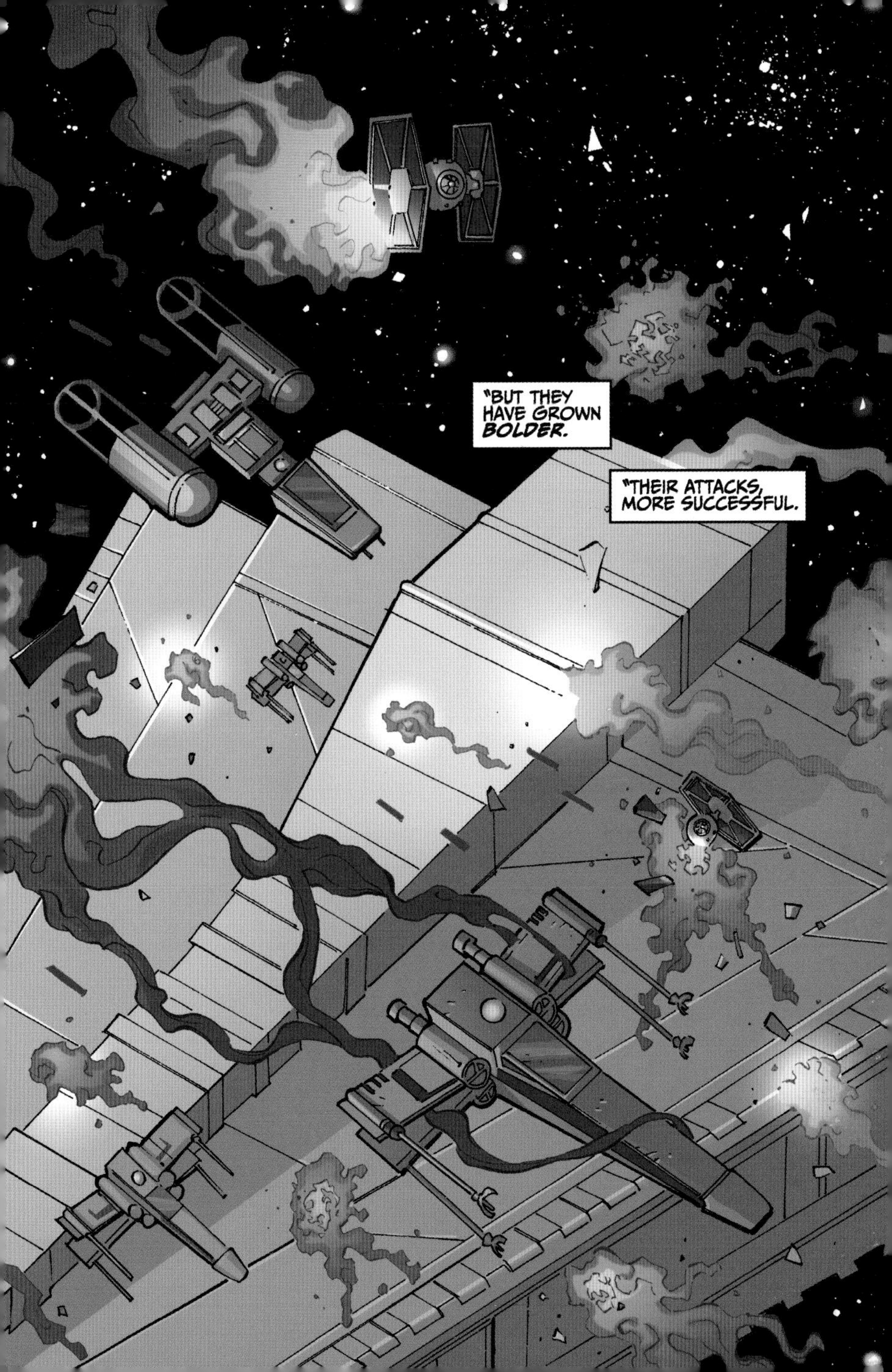
"BUT THEY HAVE GROWN BOLDER.
"THEIR ATTACKS, MORE SUCCESSFUL.

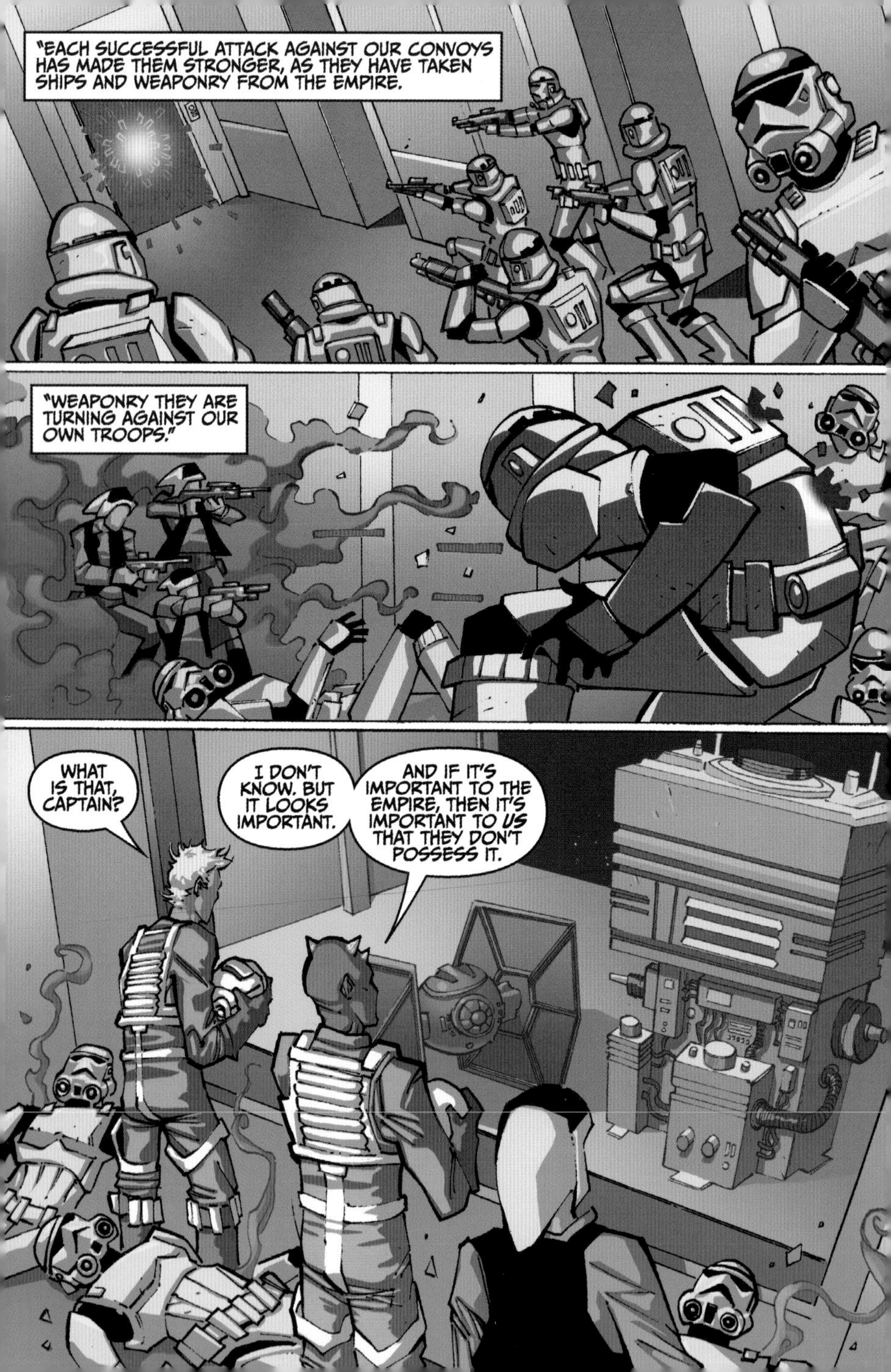
"EACH SUCCESSFUL ATTACK AGAINST OUR CONVOYS HAS MADE THEM STRONGER, AS THEY HAVE TAKEN SHIPS AND WEAPONRY FROM THE EMPIRE.
"WEAPONRY THEY ARE TURNING AGAINST OUR OWN TROOPS."
WHAT IS THAT, CAPTAIN?
I DON'T KNOW. BUT IT LOOKS IMPORTANT.
AND IF IT'S IMPORTANT TO THE EMPIRE, THEN IT'S IMPORTANT TO US THAT THEY DON'T POSSESS IT.

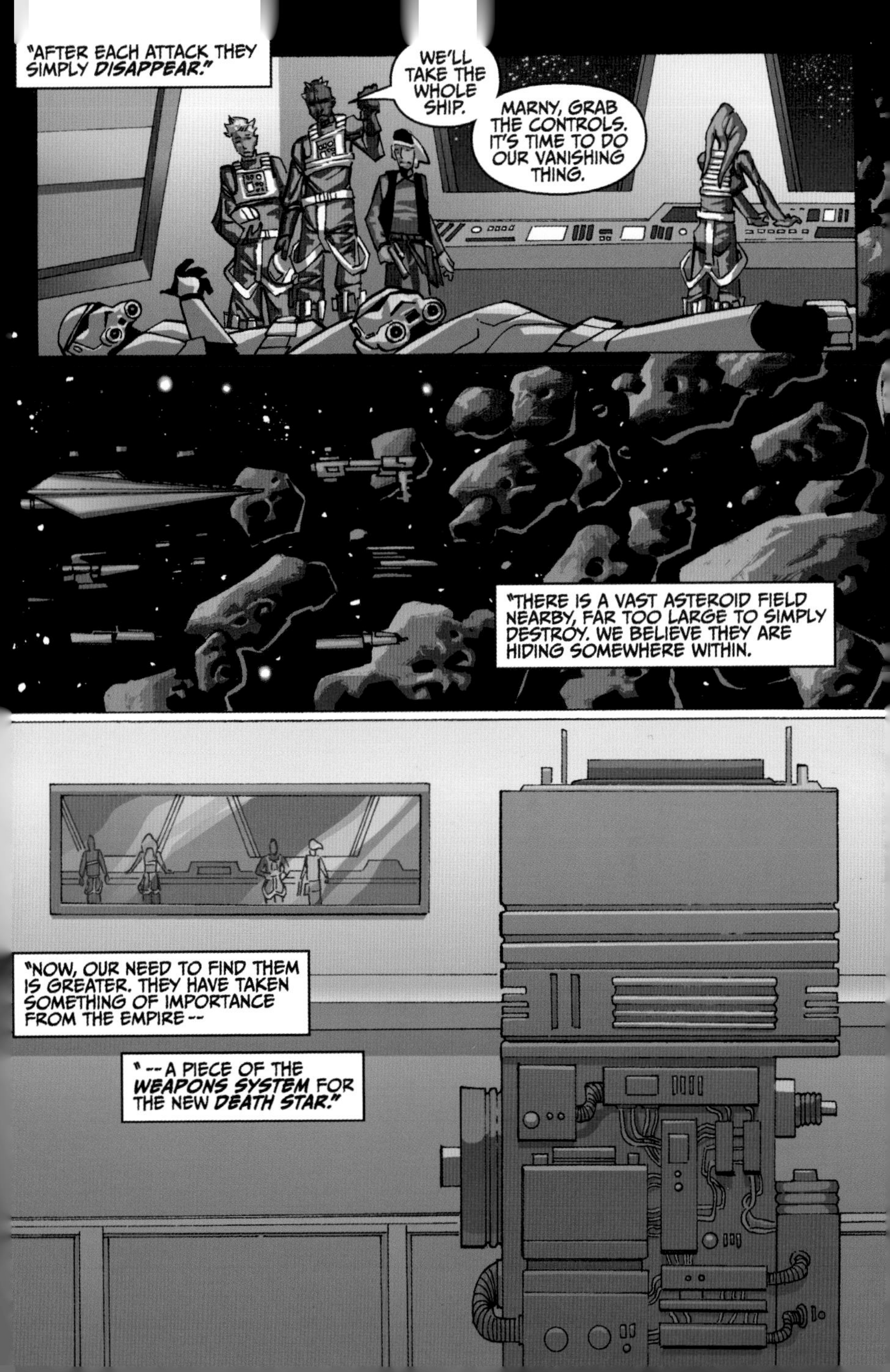
"AFTER EACH ATTACK THEY SIMPLY DISAPPEAR."
WE'LL TAKE THE WHOLE SHIP.
MARNY, GRAB THE CONTROLS. IT'S TIME TO DO OUR VANISHING THING.
"THERE IS A VAST ASTEROID FIELD NEARBY, FAR TOO LARGE TO SIMPLY DESTROY. WE BELIEVE THEY ARE HIDING SOMEWHERE WITHIN.
"NOW, OUR NEED TO FIND THEM IS GREATER. THEY HAVE TAKEN SOMETHING OF IMPORTANCE FROM THE EMPIRE--
"--A PIECE OF THE WEAPONS SYSTEM FOR THE NEW DEATH STAR."

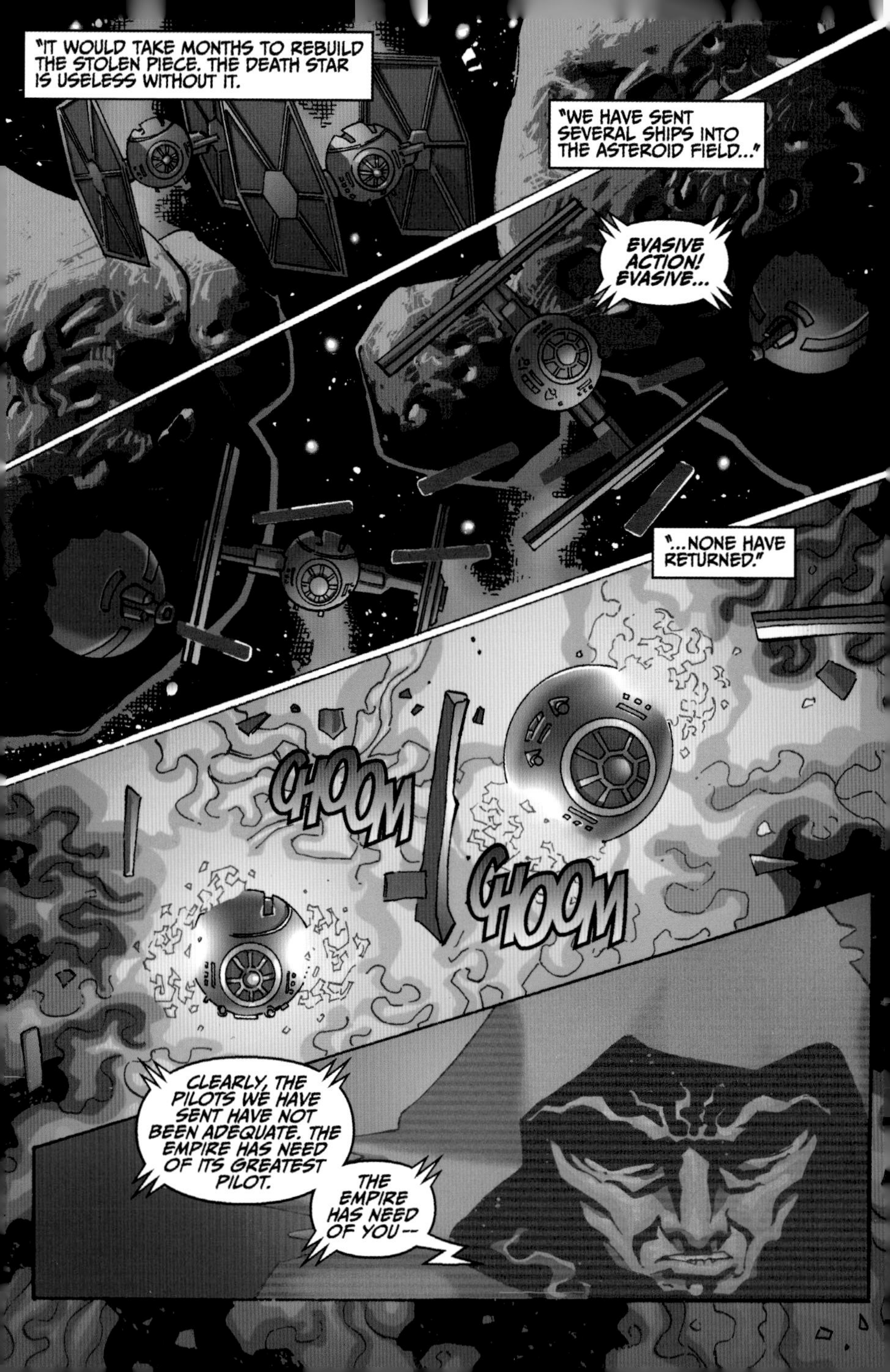
"IT WOULD TAKE MONTHS TO REBUILD THE STOLEN PIECE. THE DEATH STAR IS USELESS WITHOUT IT.
"WE HAVE SENT SEVERAL SHIPS INTO THE ASTEROID FIELD..."
EVASIVE ACTION! EVASIVE...
"...NONE HAVE RETURNED."
CHOOM
CHOOM
CLEARLY, THE PILOTS WE HAVE SENT HAVE NOT BEEN ADEQUATE. THE EMPIRE HAS NEED OF ITS GREATEST PILOT.
THE EMPIRE HAS NEED OF YOU --

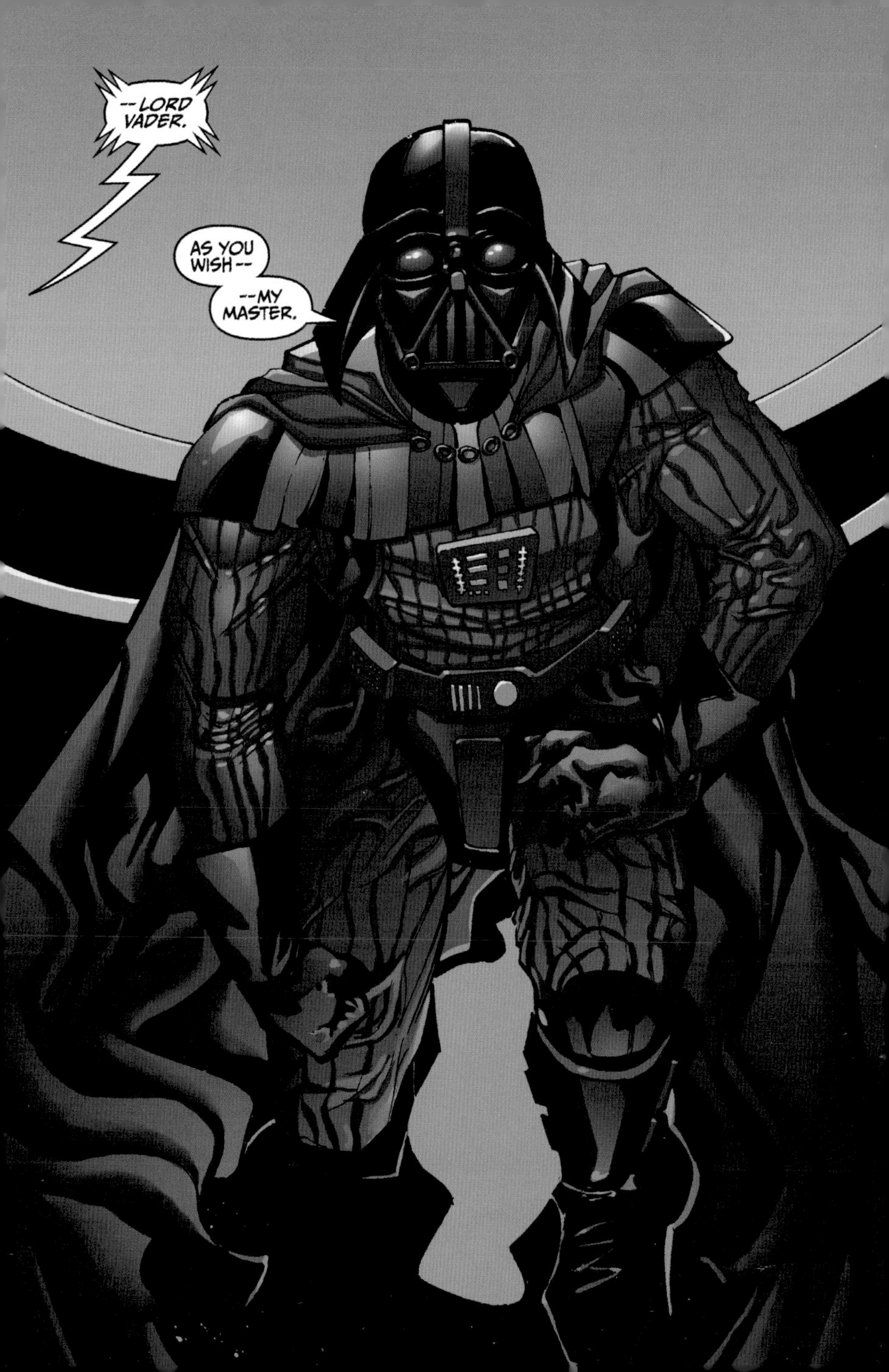
--LORD VADER.
AS YOU WISH--
--MY MASTER.

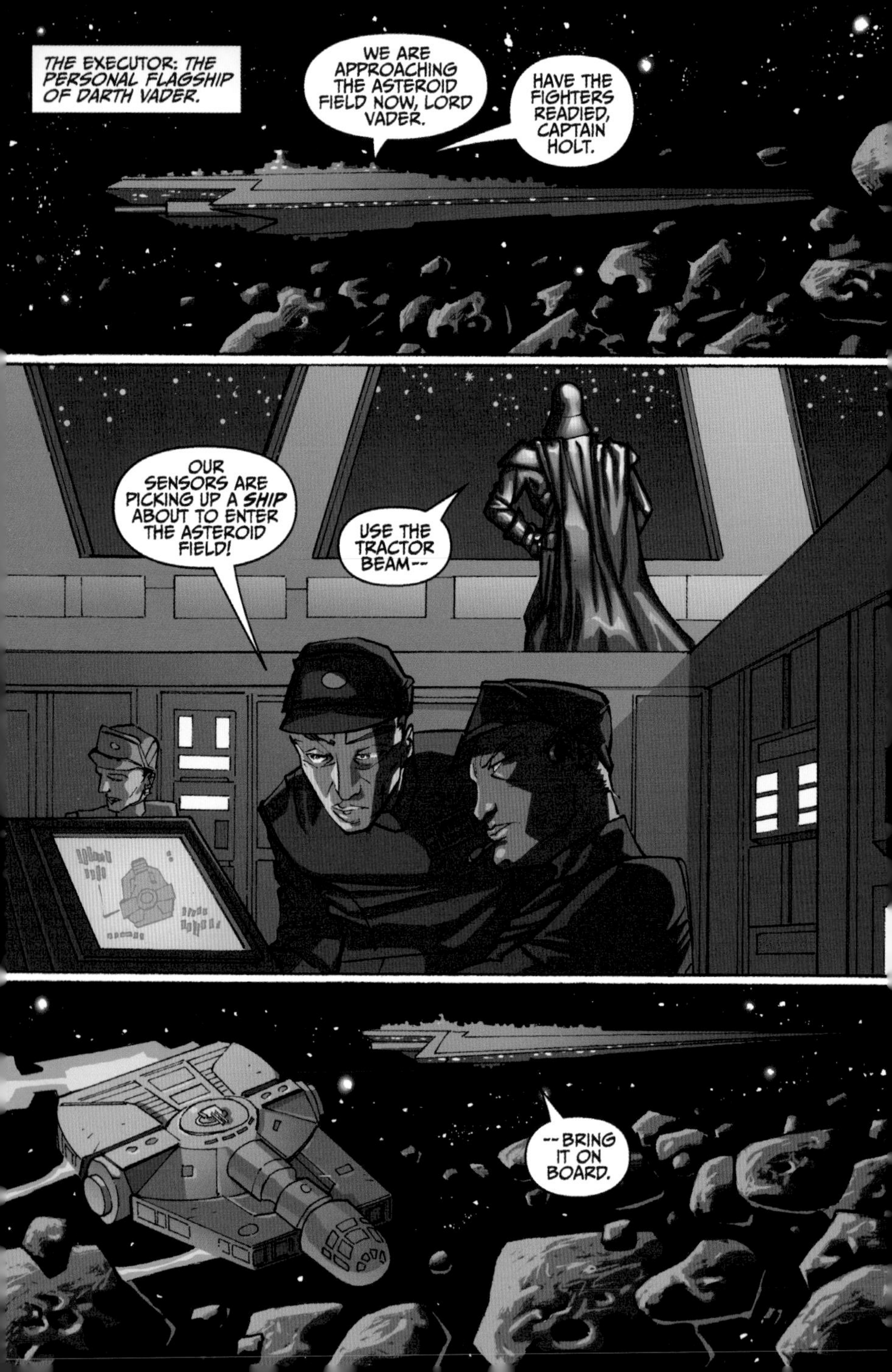
THE EXECUTOR: THE PERSONAL FLAGSHIP OF DARTH VADER.
WE ARE APPROACHING THE ASTEROID FIELD NOW, LORD VADER.
HAVE THE FIGHTERS READIED, CAPTAIN HOLT.
OUR SENSORS ARE PICKING UP A *SHIP* ABOUT TO ENTER THE ASTEROID FIELD!
USE THE TRACTOR BEAM--
--BRING IT ON BOARD.

SHIP'S CREW. YOU WILL EXIT YOUR VESSEL WITH YOUR HANDS RAISED.
UH-OH!

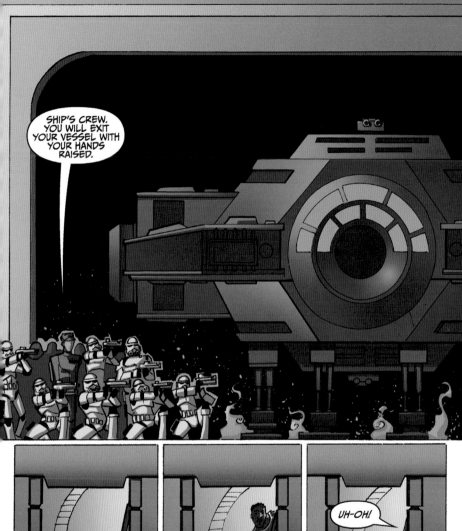

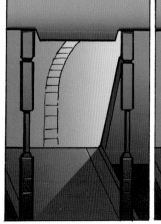

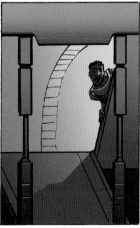

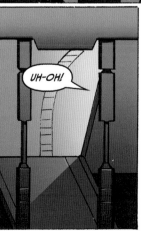

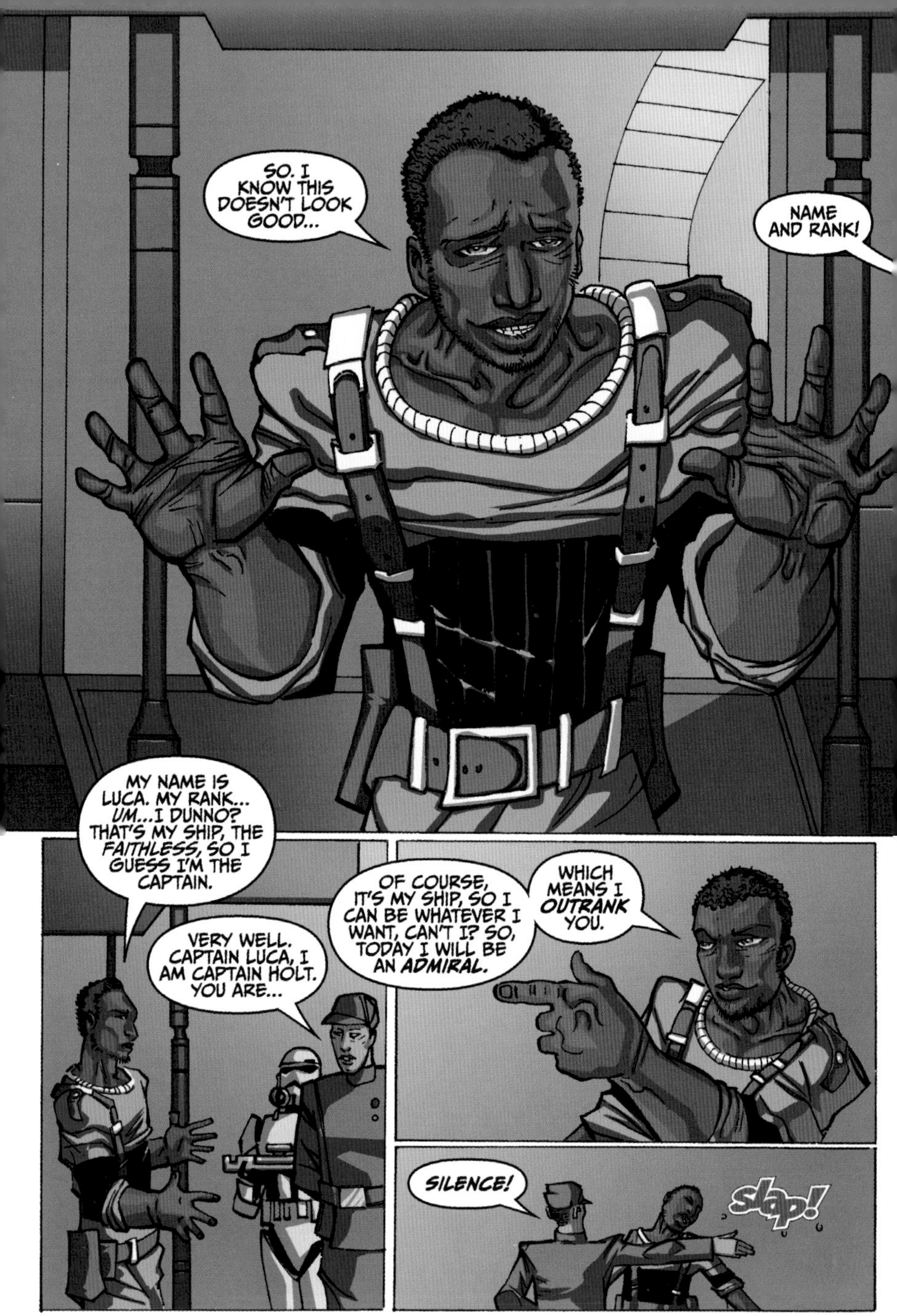
SO. I KNOW THIS DOESN'T LOOK GOOD...
NAME AND RANK!
MY NAME IS LUCA. MY RANK... *UM*...I DUNNO? THAT'S MY SHIP, THE *FAITHLESS*, SO I GUESS I'M THE CAPTAIN.
VERY WELL. CAPTAIN LUCA, I AM CAPTAIN HOLT. YOU ARE...
OF COURSE, IT'S MY SHIP, SO I CAN BE WHATEVER I WANT, CAN'T I? SO, TODAY I WILL BE AN ***ADMIRAL.***
WHICH MEANS I ***OUTRANK*** YOU.
SILENCE!
SLAP!

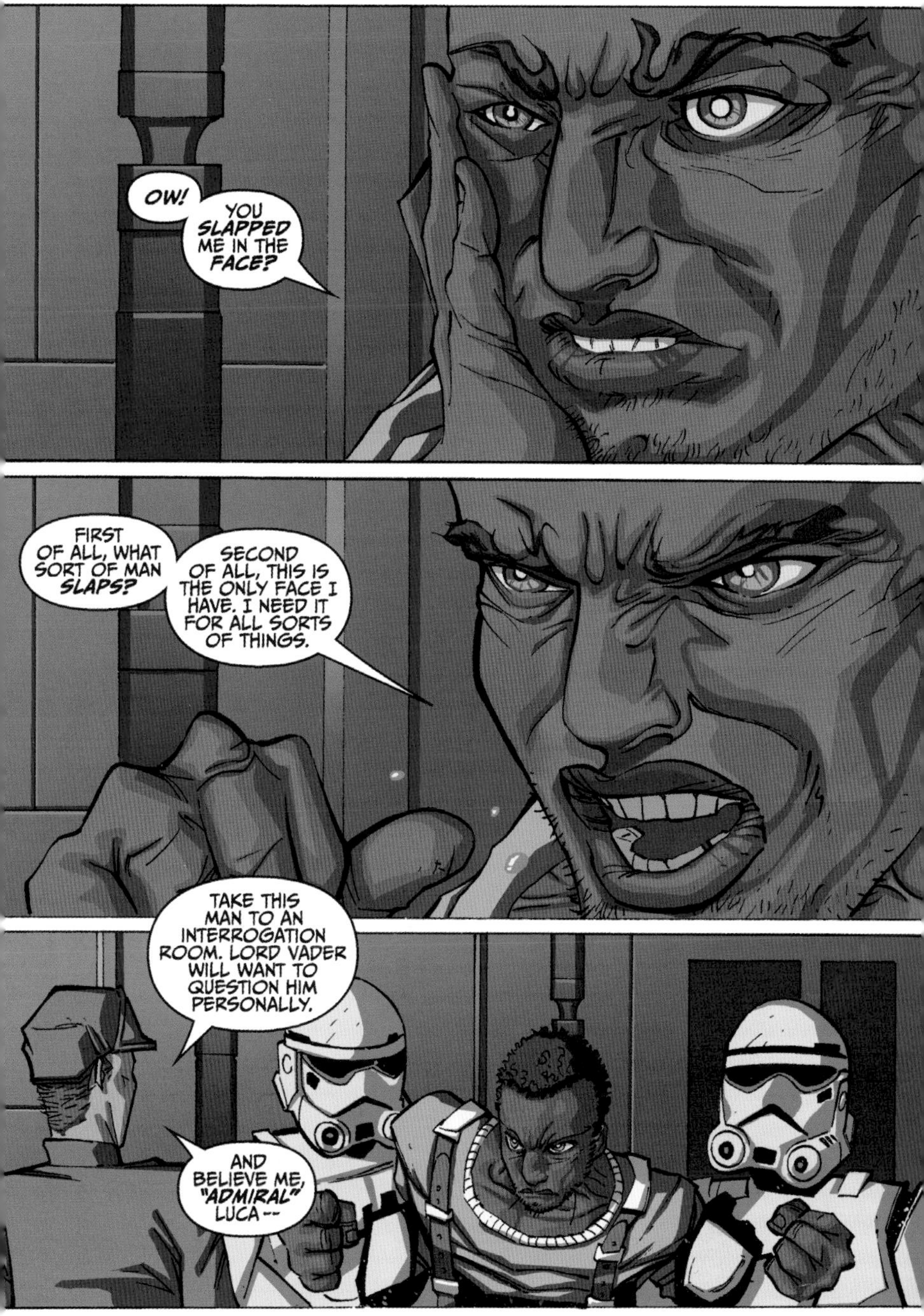
OW!
YOU *SLAPPED* ME IN THE *FACE?*
FIRST OF ALL, WHAT SORT OF MAN *SLAPS?*
SECOND OF ALL, THIS IS THE ONLY FACE I HAVE. I NEED IT FOR ALL SORTS OF THINGS.
TAKE THIS MAN TO AN INTERROGATION ROOM. LORD VADER WILL WANT TO QUESTION HIM PERSONALLY.
AND BELIEVE ME, *"ADMIRAL"* LUCA --

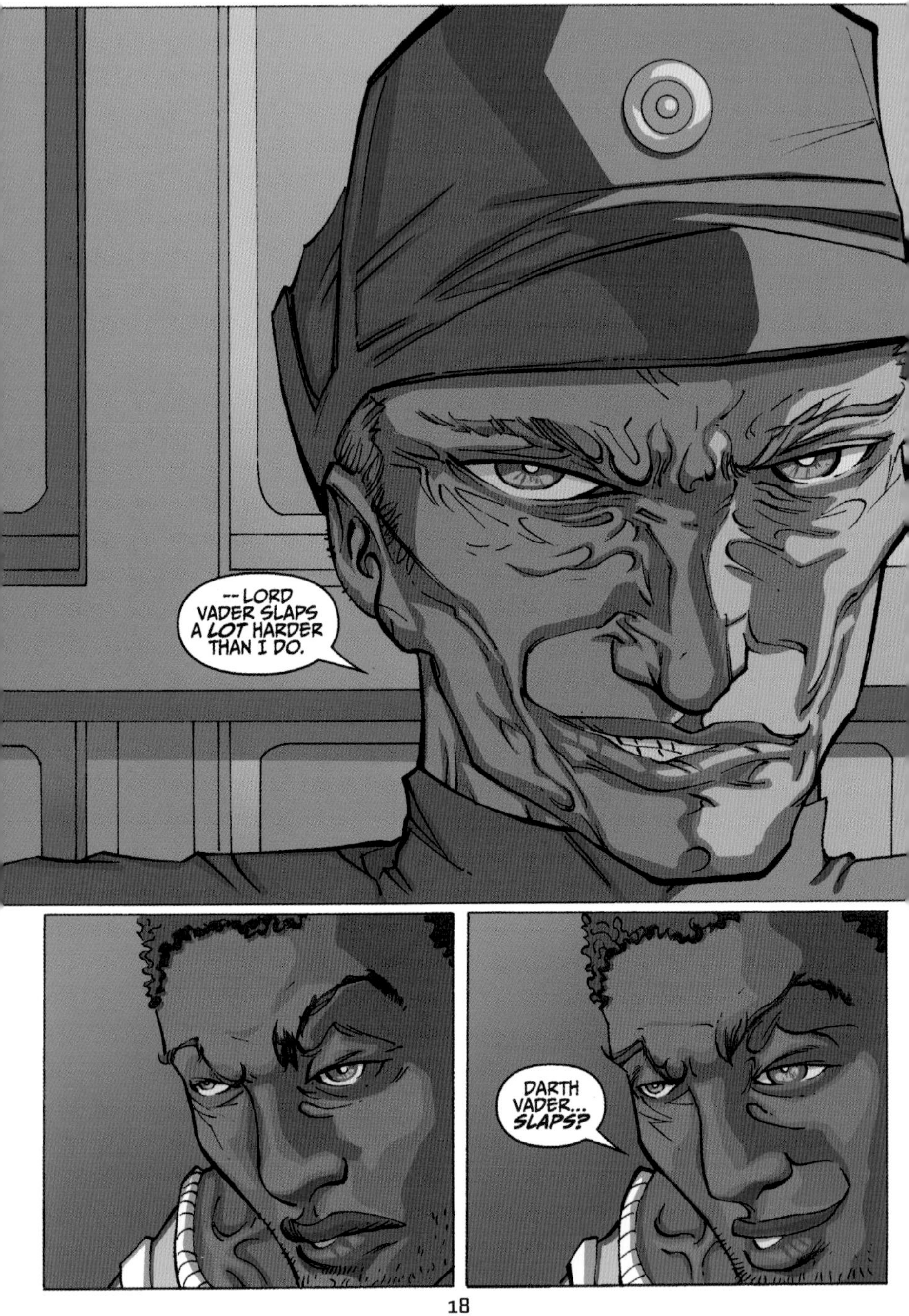
--LORD VADER SLAPS A *LOT* HARDER THAN I DO.
DARTH VADER... *SLAPS?*

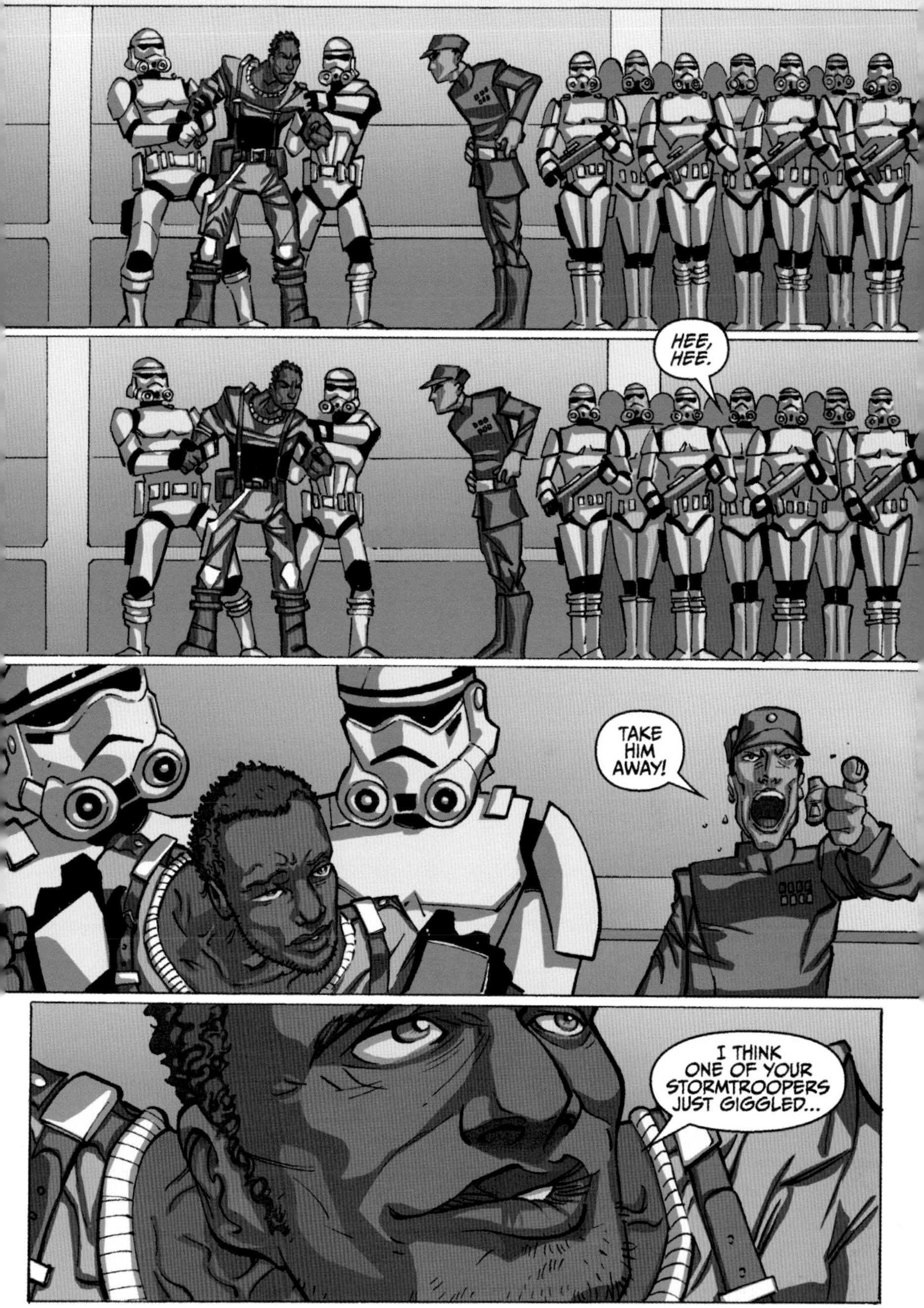
HEE, HEE.
TAKE HIM AWAY!
I THINK ONE OF YOUR STORMTROOPERS JUST GIGGLED...

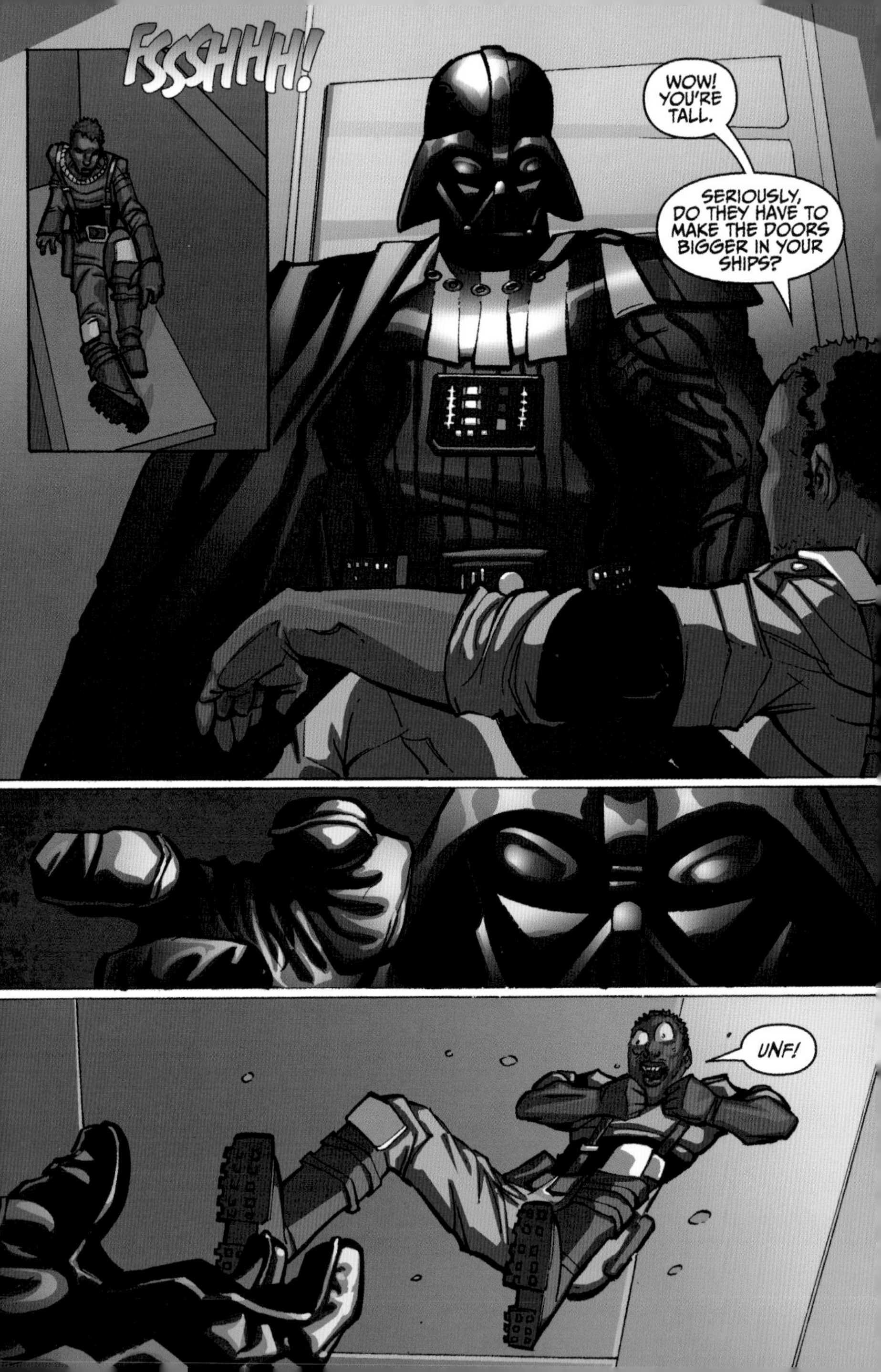
FSSSHHH!
WOW! YOU'RE TALL.
SERIOUSLY, DO THEY HAVE TO MAKE THE DOORS BIGGER IN YOUR SHIPS?
UNF!

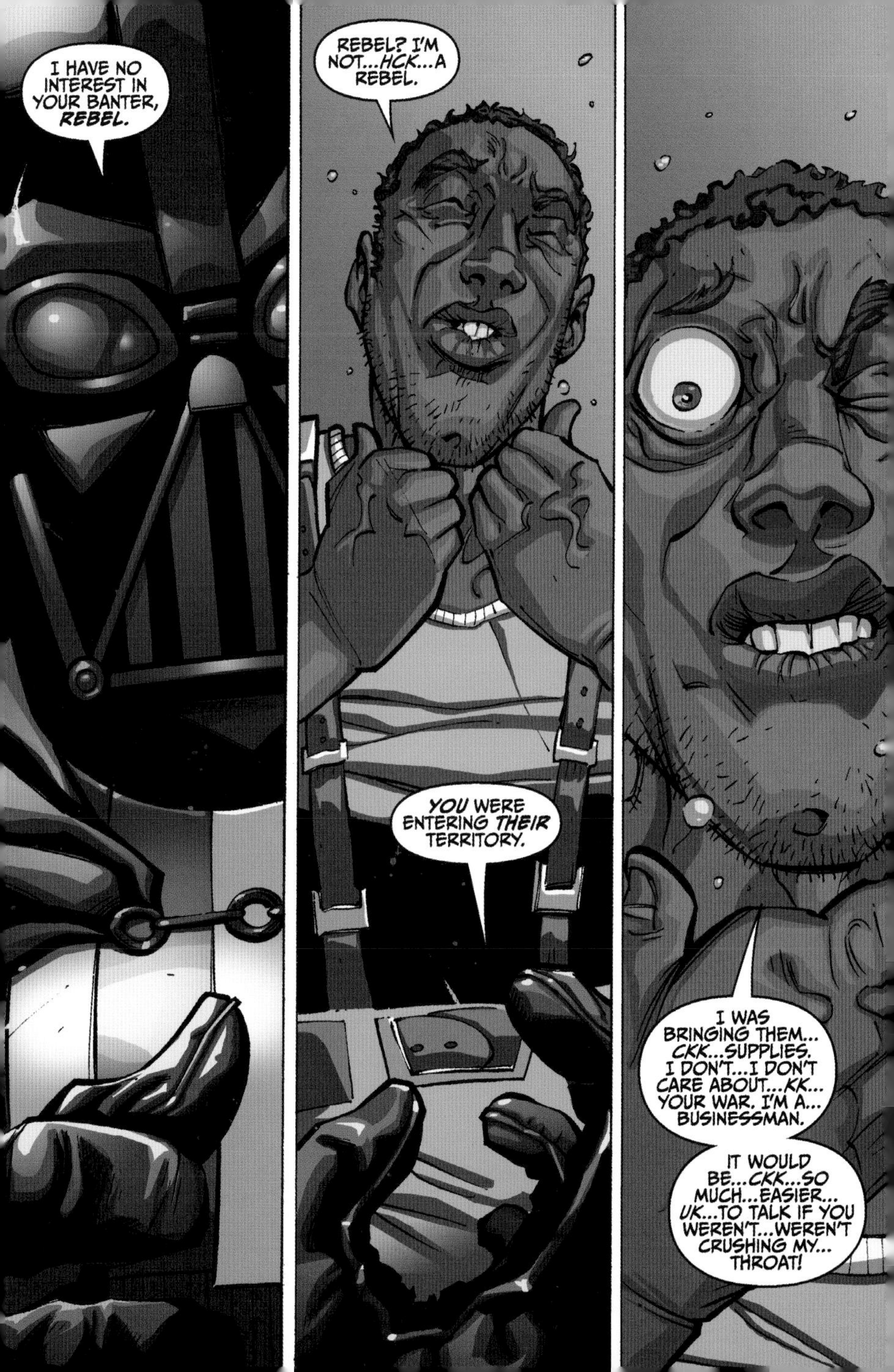
I HAVE NO INTEREST IN YOUR BANTER, *REBEL.*
REBEL? I'M NOT...*HCK*...A REBEL.
YOU WERE ENTERING *THEIR* TERRITORY.
I WAS BRINGING THEM... *CKK*...SUPPLIES. I DON'T...I DON'T CARE ABOUT...*KK*... YOUR WAR. I'M A... BUSINESSMAN.
IT WOULD BE...*CKK*...SO MUCH...EASIER... *UK*...TO TALK IF YOU WEREN'T...WEREN'T CRUSHING MY... THROAT!

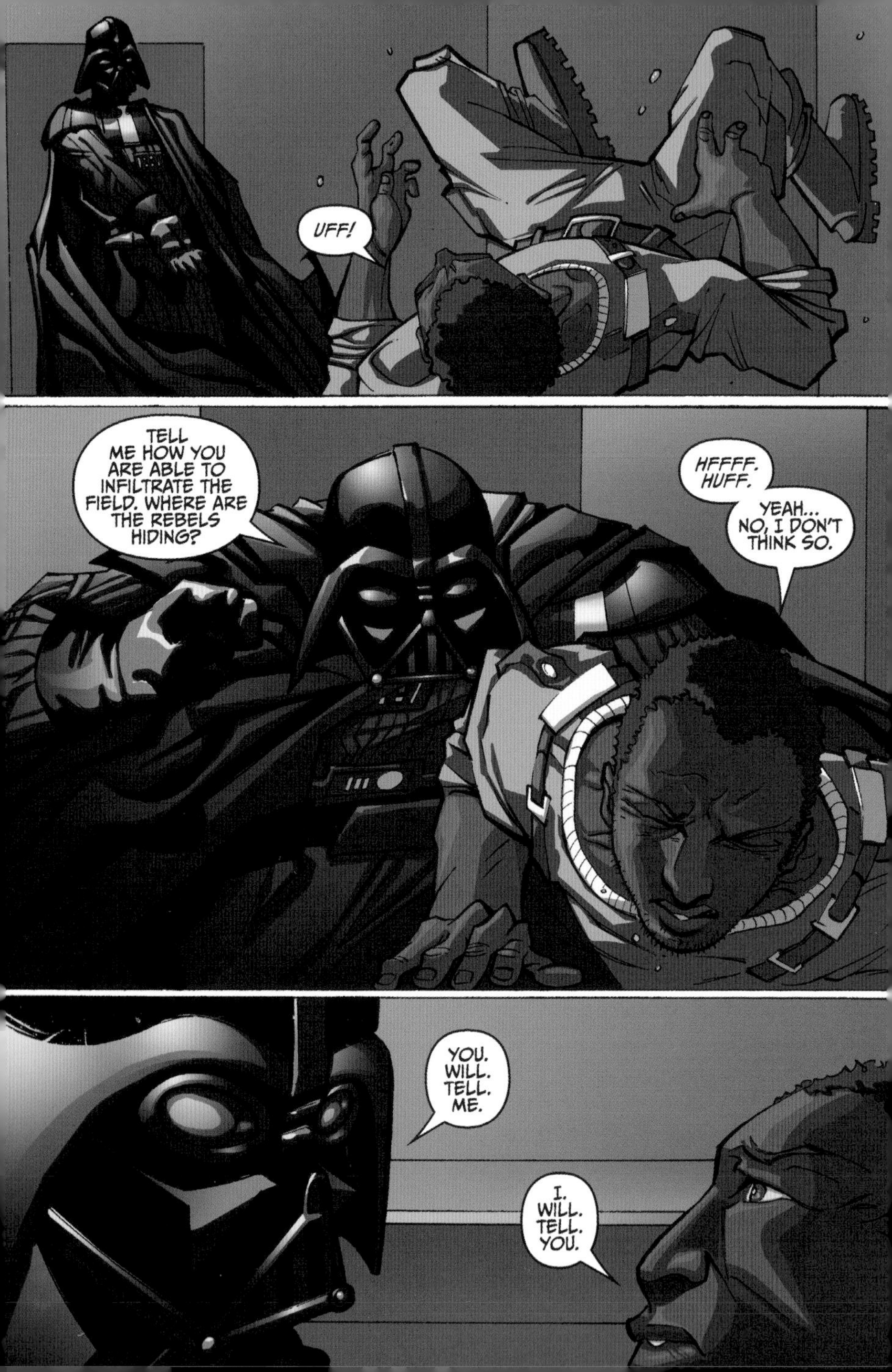
UFF!
TELL ME HOW YOU ARE ABLE TO INFILTRATE THE FIELD. WHERE ARE THE REBELS HIDING?
HFFFF. HUFF.
YEAH... NO, I DON'T THINK SO.
YOU. WILL. TELL. ME.
I. WILL. TELL. YOU.

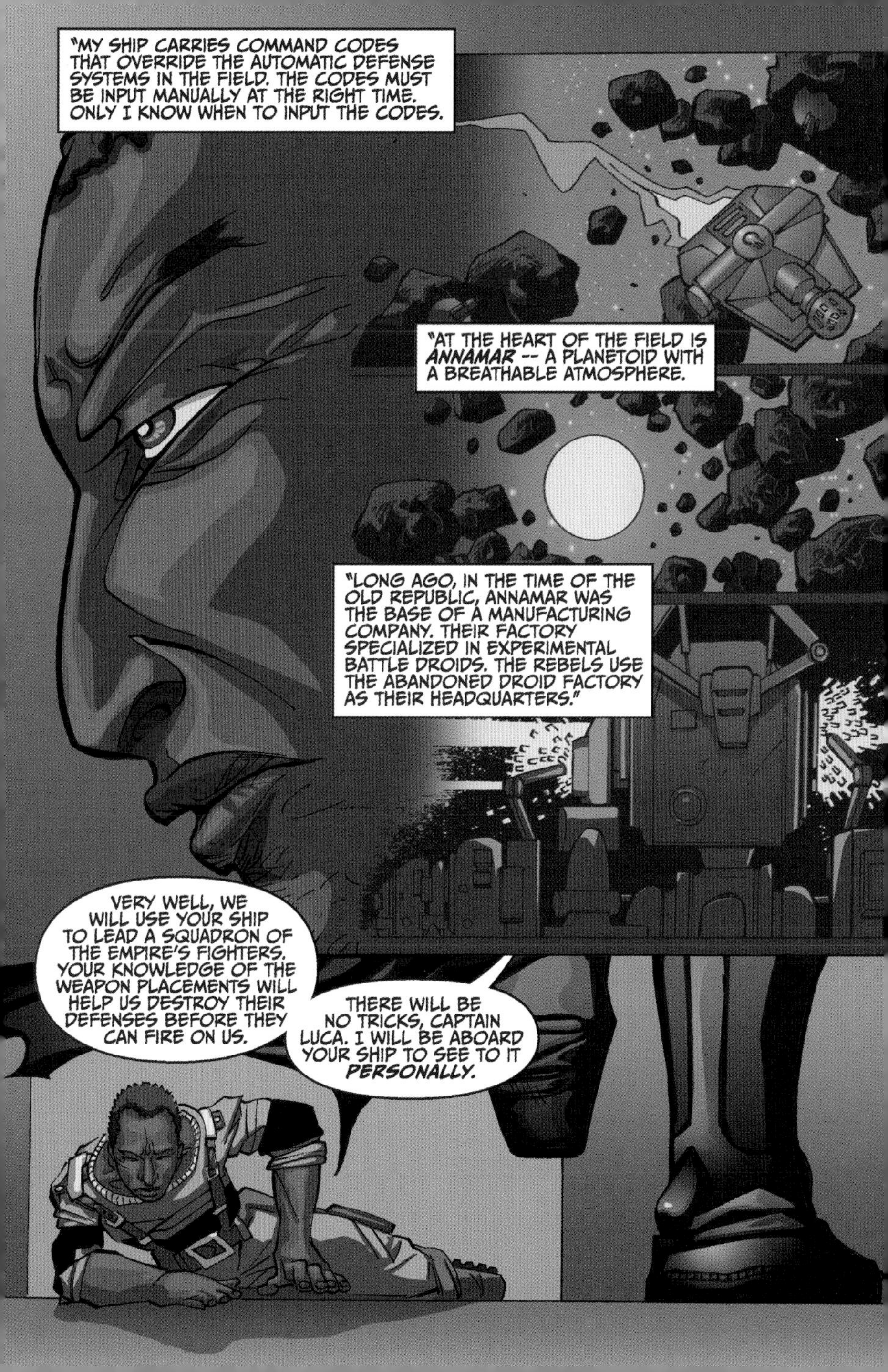
"MY SHIP CARRIES COMMAND CODES THAT OVERRIDE THE AUTOMATIC DEFENSE SYSTEMS IN THE FIELD. THE CODES MUST BE INPUT MANUALLY AT THE RIGHT TIME. ONLY I KNOW WHEN TO INPUT THE CODES.
"AT THE HEART OF THE FIELD IS *ANNAMAR* -- A PLANETOID WITH A BREATHABLE ATMOSPHERE.
"LONG AGO, IN THE TIME OF THE OLD REPUBLIC, ANNAMAR WAS THE BASE OF A MANUFACTURING COMPANY. THEIR FACTORY SPECIALIZED IN EXPERIMENTAL BATTLE DROIDS. THE REBELS USE THE ABANDONED DROID FACTORY AS THEIR HEADQUARTERS."
VERY WELL, WE WILL USE YOUR SHIP TO LEAD A SQUADRON OF THE EMPIRE'S FIGHTERS. YOUR KNOWLEDGE OF THE WEAPON PLACEMENTS WILL HELP US DESTROY THEIR DEFENSES BEFORE THEY CAN FIRE ON US.
THERE WILL BE NO TRICKS, CAPTAIN LUCA. I WILL BE ABOARD YOUR SHIP TO SEE TO IT *PERSONALLY.*

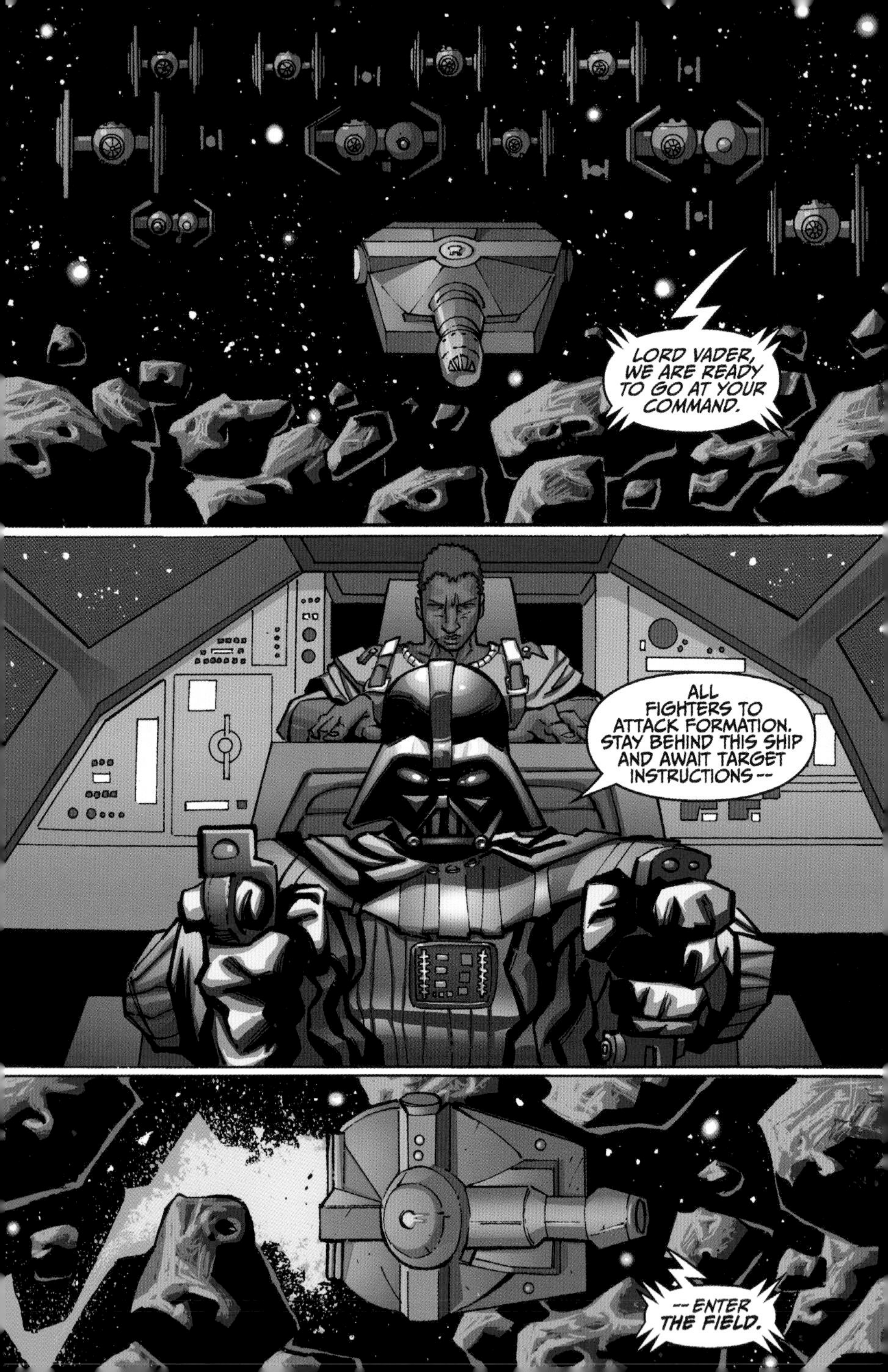
LORD VADER, WE ARE READY TO GO AT YOUR COMMAND.
ALL FIGHTERS TO ATTACK FORMATION. STAY BEHIND THIS SHIP AND AWAIT TARGET INSTRUCTIONS --
-- ENTER THE FIELD.

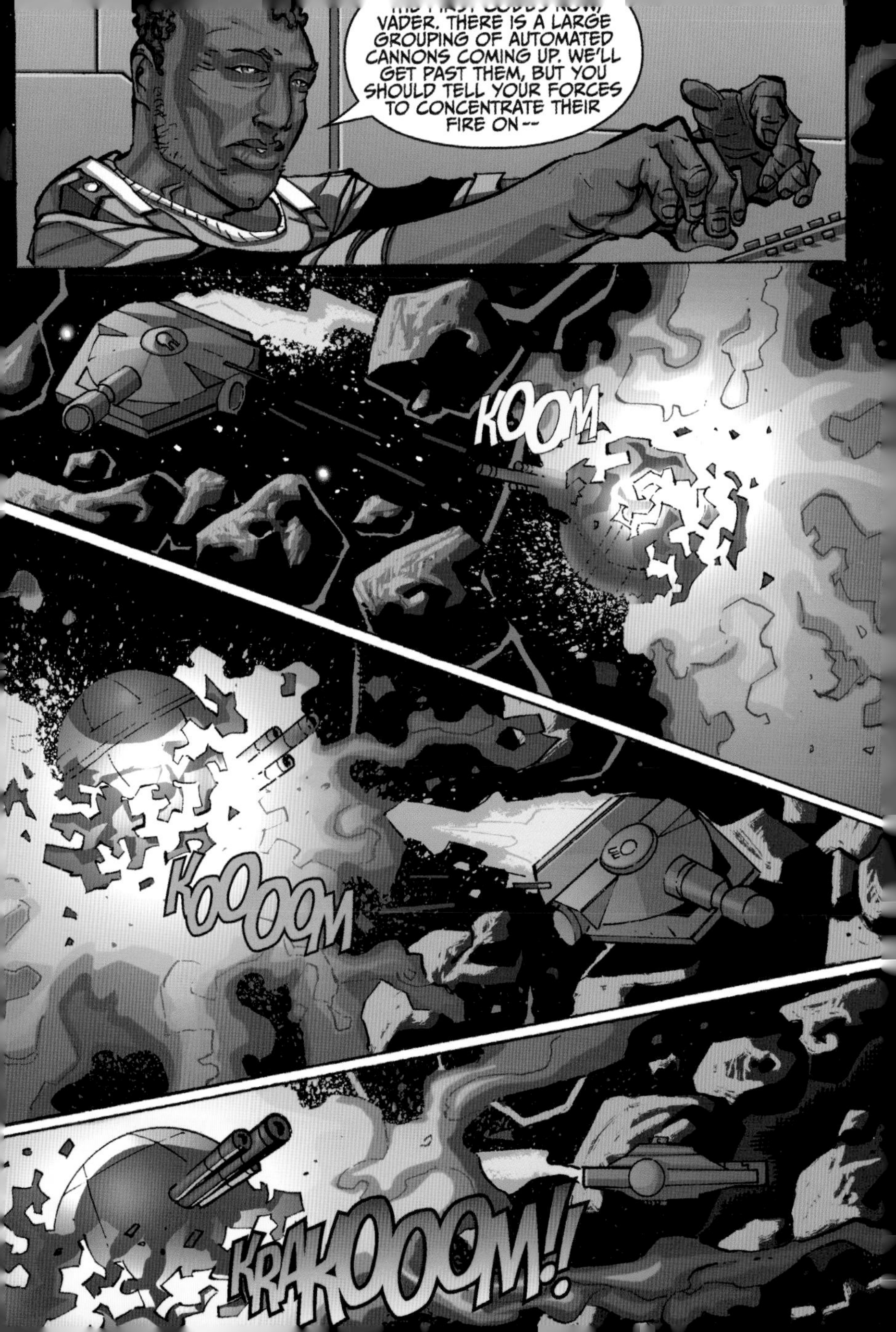
VADER. THERE IS A LARGE GROUPING OF AUTOMATED CANNONS COMING UP. WE'LL GET PAST THEM, BUT YOU SHOULD TELL YOUR FORCES TO CONCENTRATE THEIR FIRE ON--
KOOM
KOOOOM
KRAKOOOOM!!

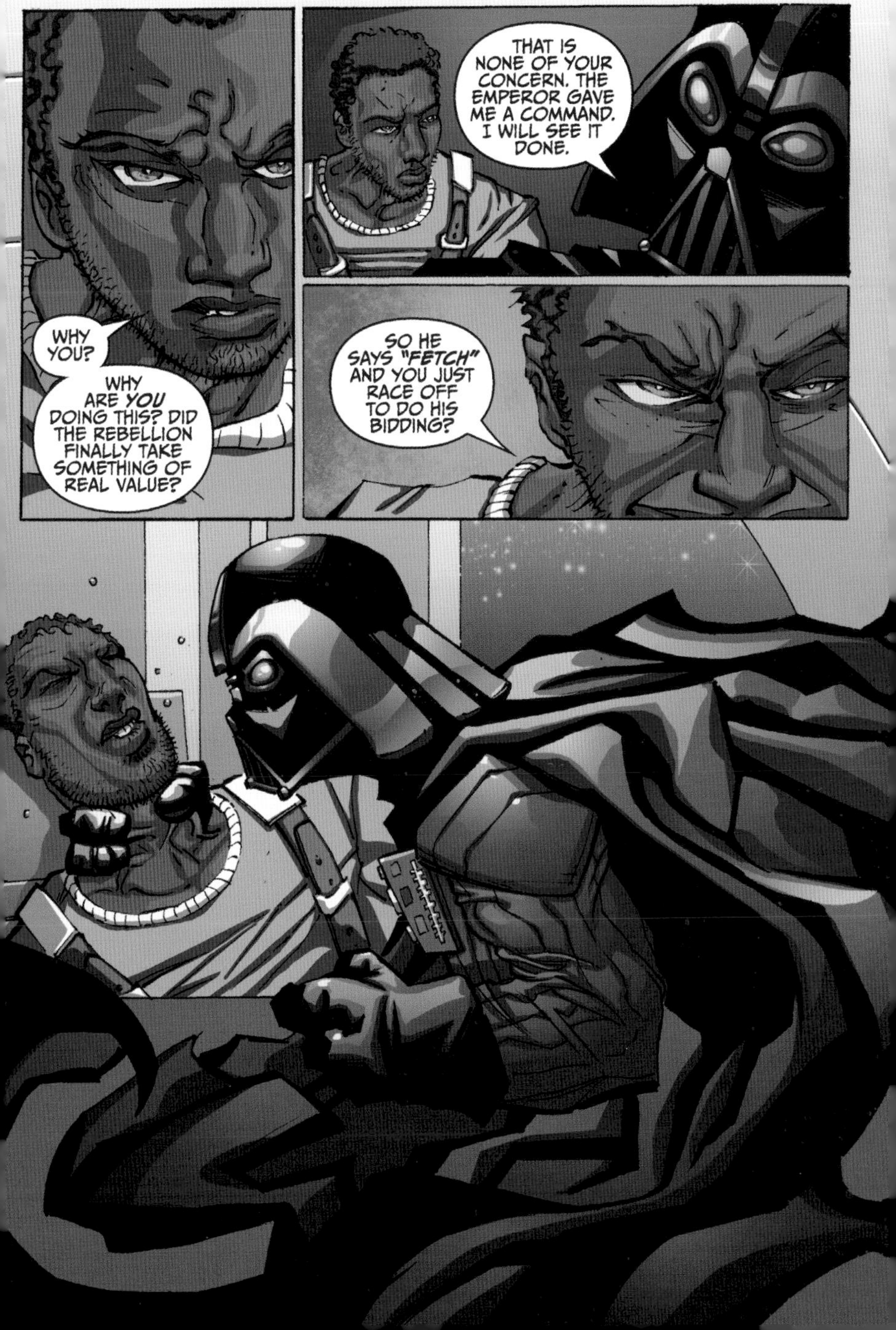
WHY YOU?
WHY ARE YOU DOING THIS? DID THE REBELLION FINALLY TAKE SOMETHING OF REAL VALUE?
THAT IS NONE OF YOUR CONCERN. THE EMPEROR GAVE ME A COMMAND. I WILL SEE IT DONE.
SO HE SAYS "FETCH" AND YOU JUST RACE OFF TO DO HIS BIDDING?

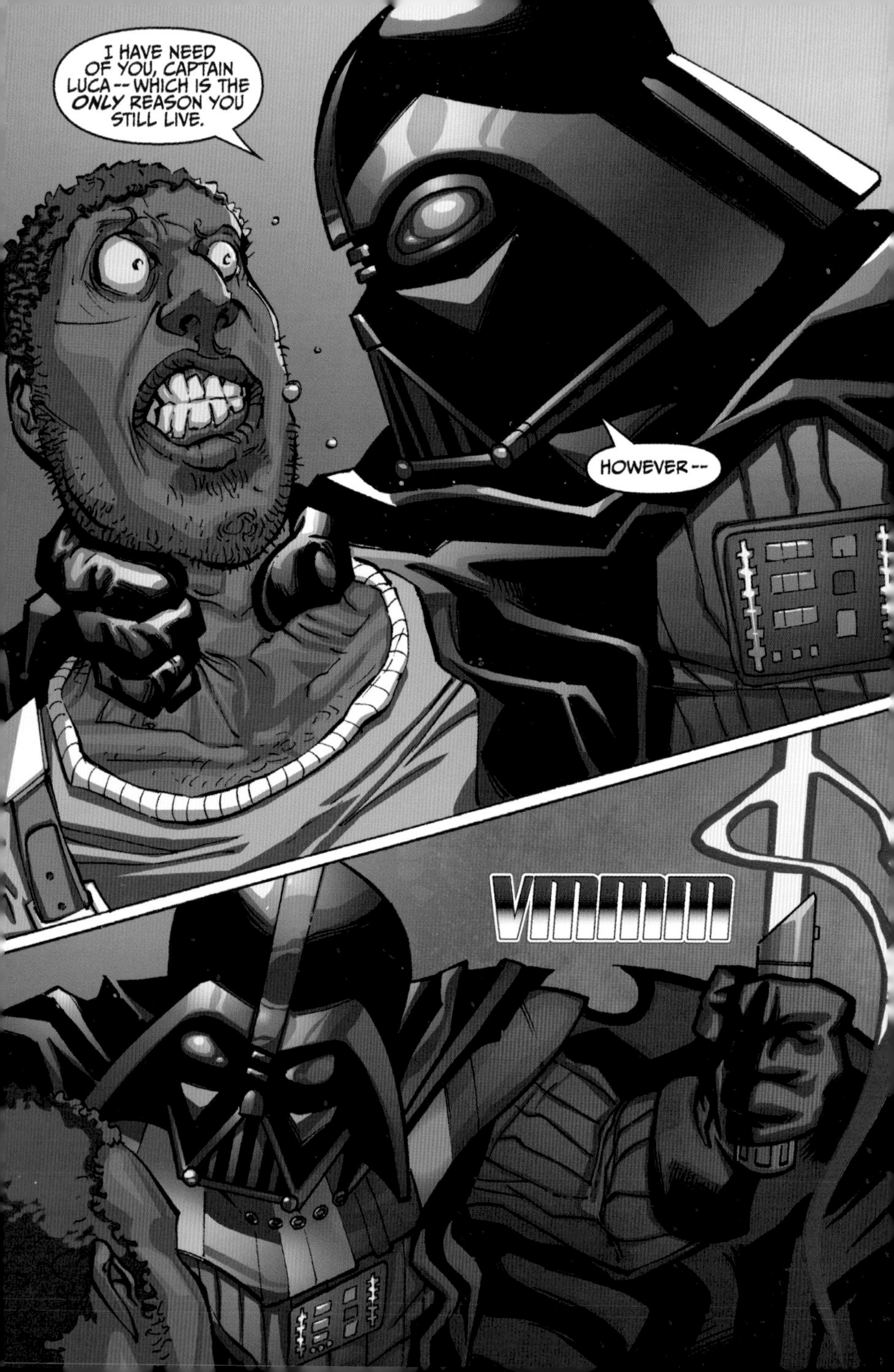
I HAVE NEED OF YOU, CAPTAIN LUCA -- WHICH IS THE *ONLY* REASON YOU STILL LIVE.
HOWEVER --
VMMM

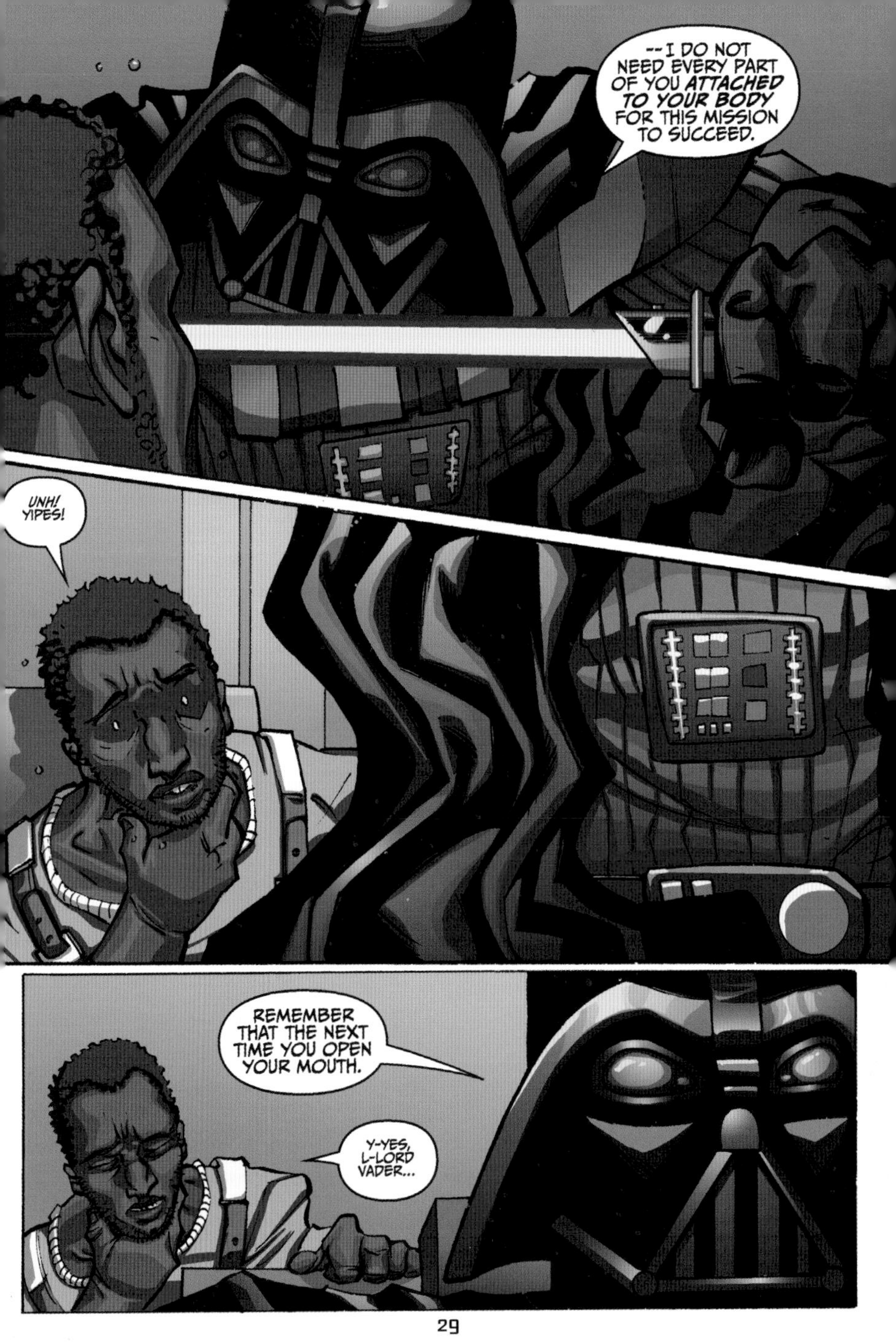
--I DO NOT NEED EVERY PART OF YOU ATTACHED TO YOUR BODY FOR THIS MISSION TO SUCCEED.
UNH! YIPES!
REMEMBER THAT THE NEXT TIME YOU OPEN YOUR MOUTH.
Y-YES, L-LORD VADER...

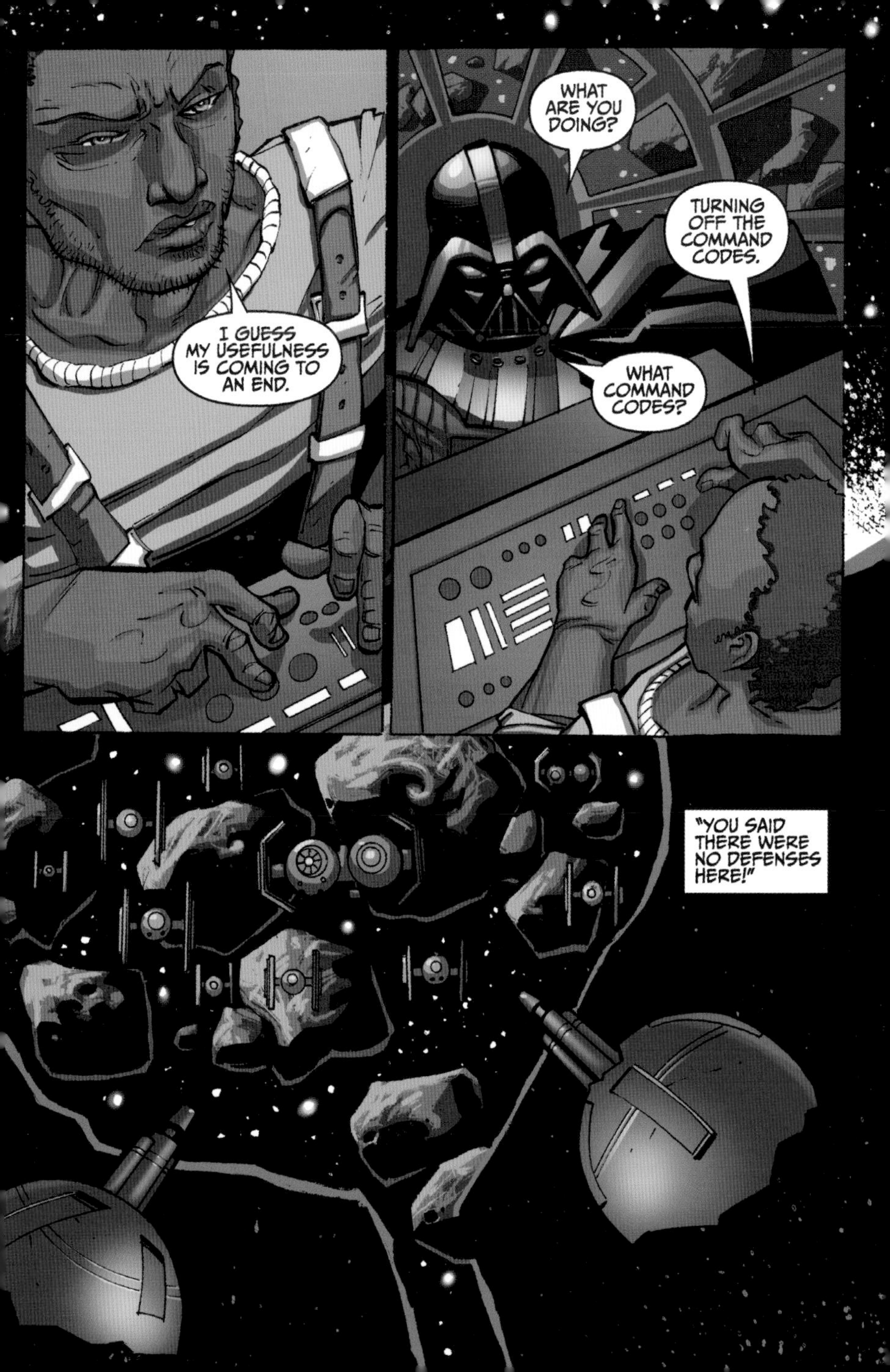
I GUESS MY USEFULNESS IS COMING TO AN END.
WHAT ARE YOU DOING?
TURNING OFF THE COMMAND CODES.
WHAT COMMAND CODES?
"YOU SAID THERE WERE NO DEFENSES HERE!"

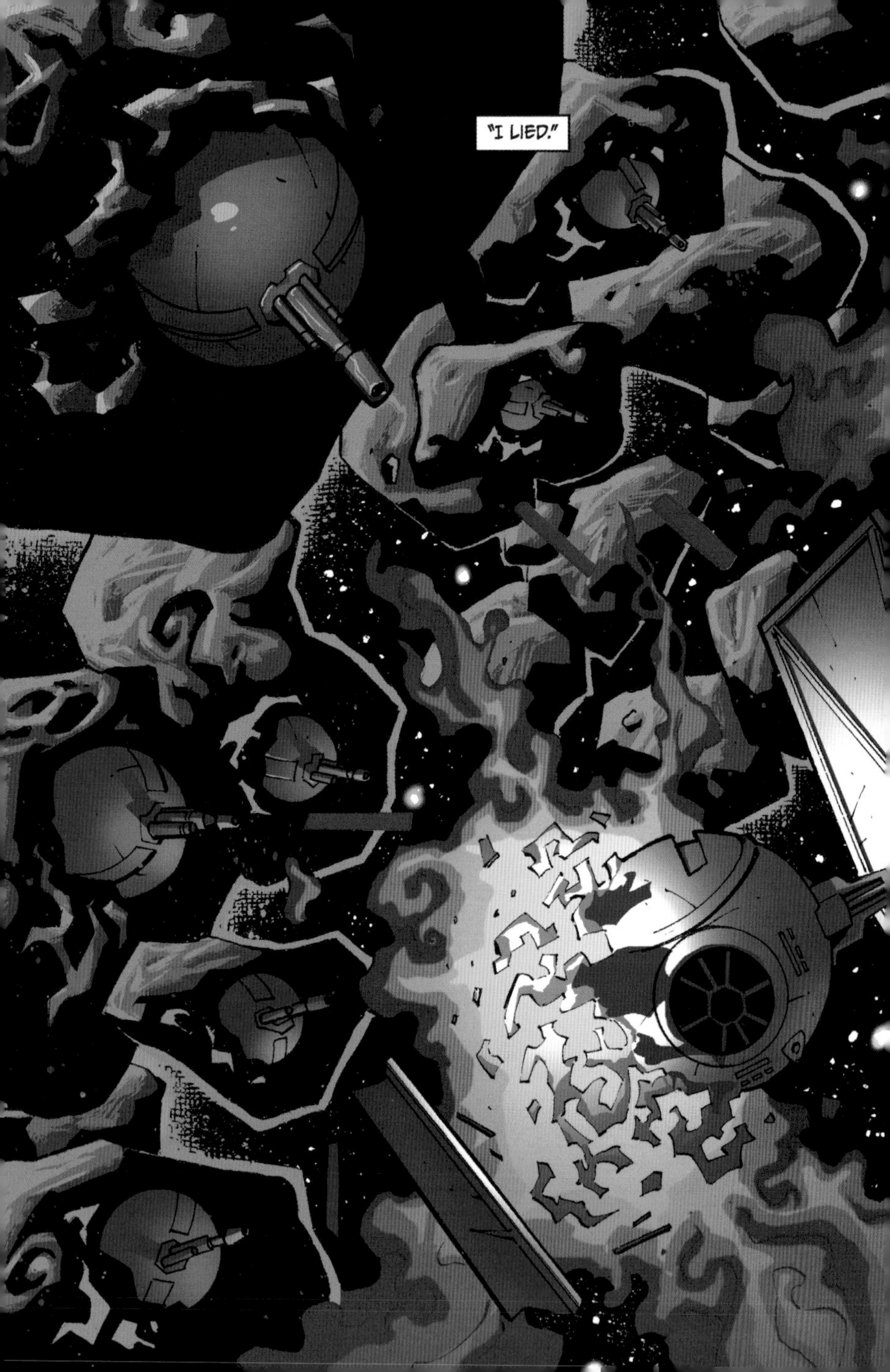
"I LIED."

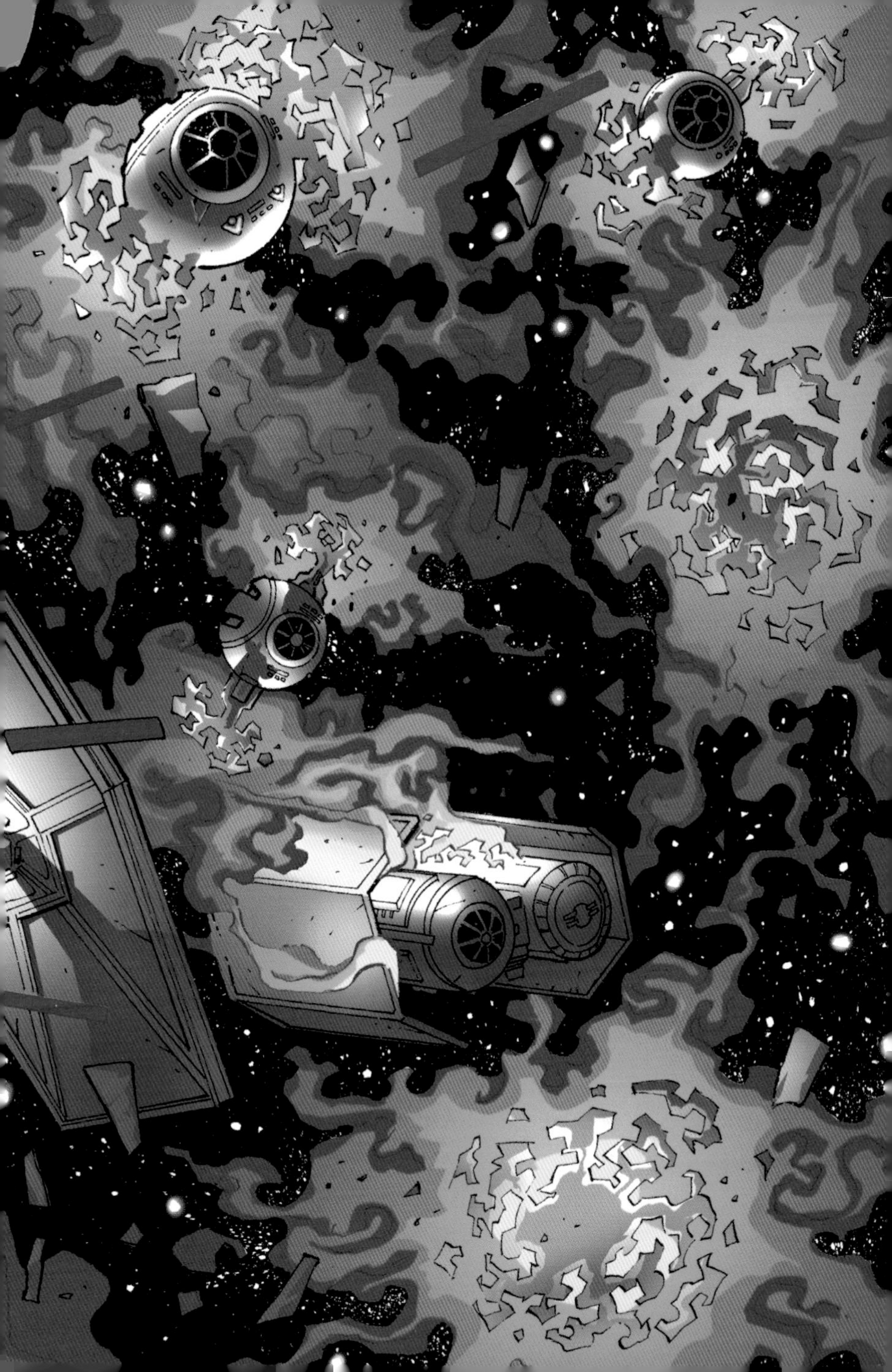

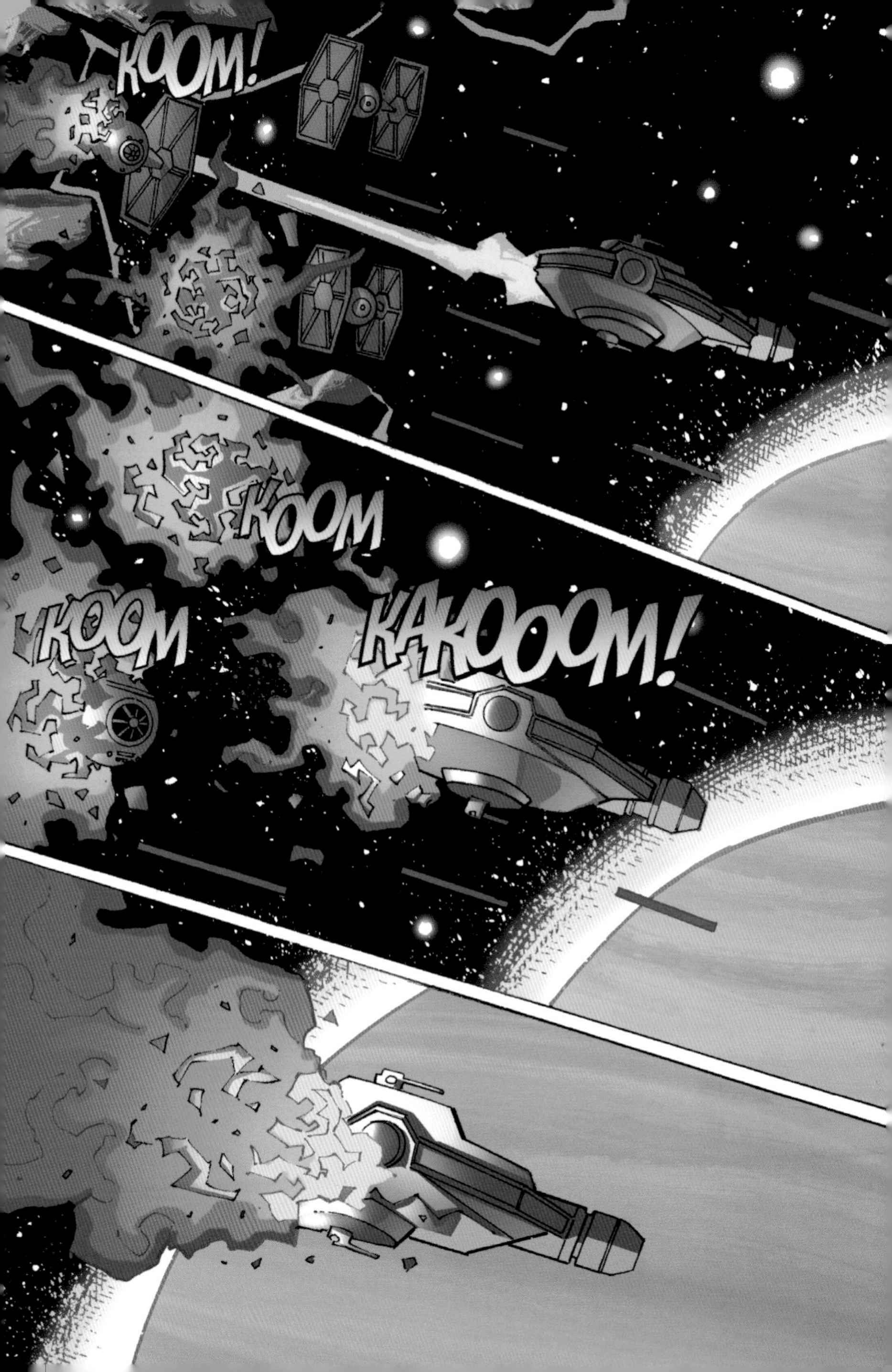
KOOM!
KOOM
KOOM
KAKOOOM!

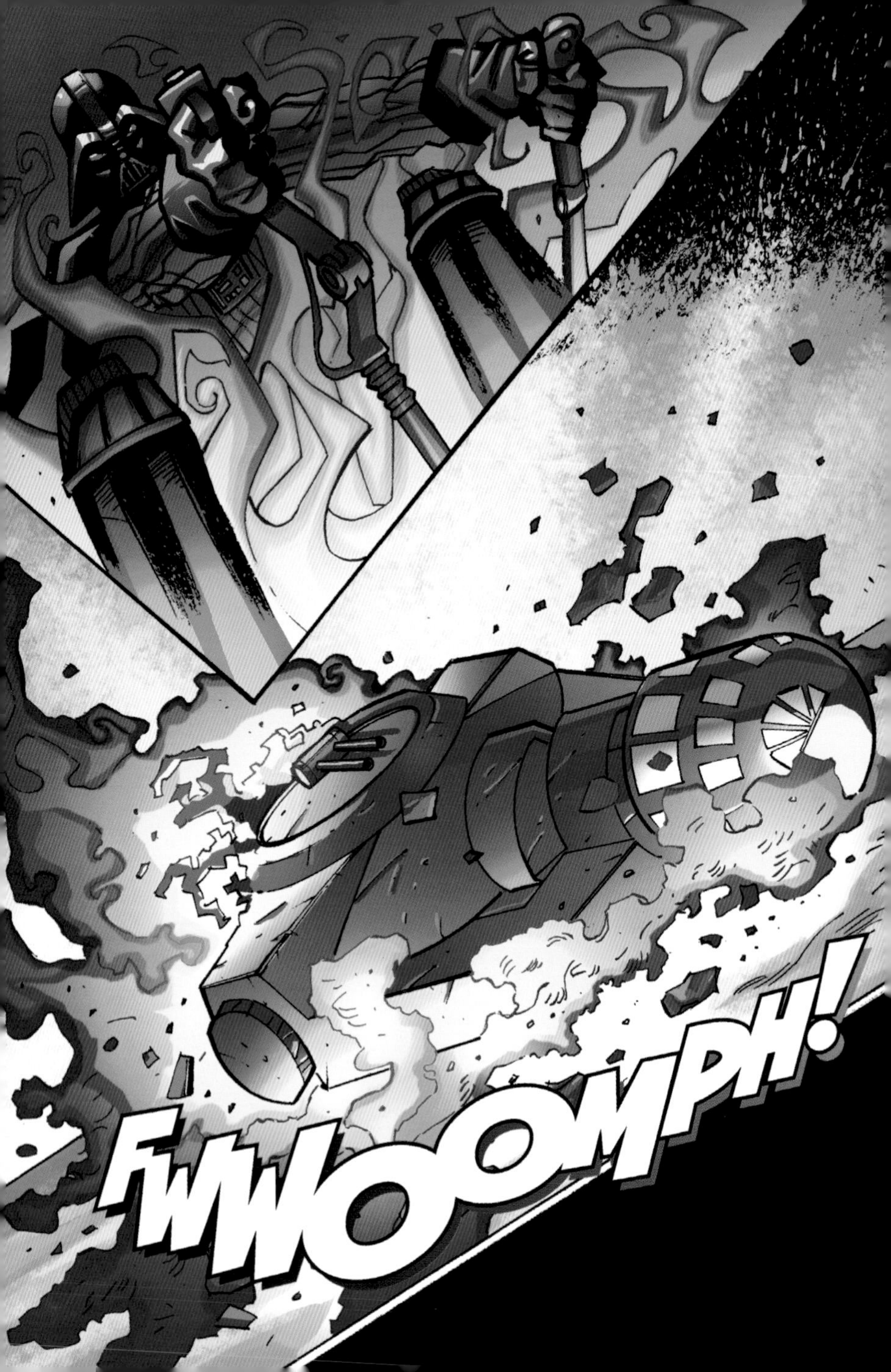
FWWOOOMPH!

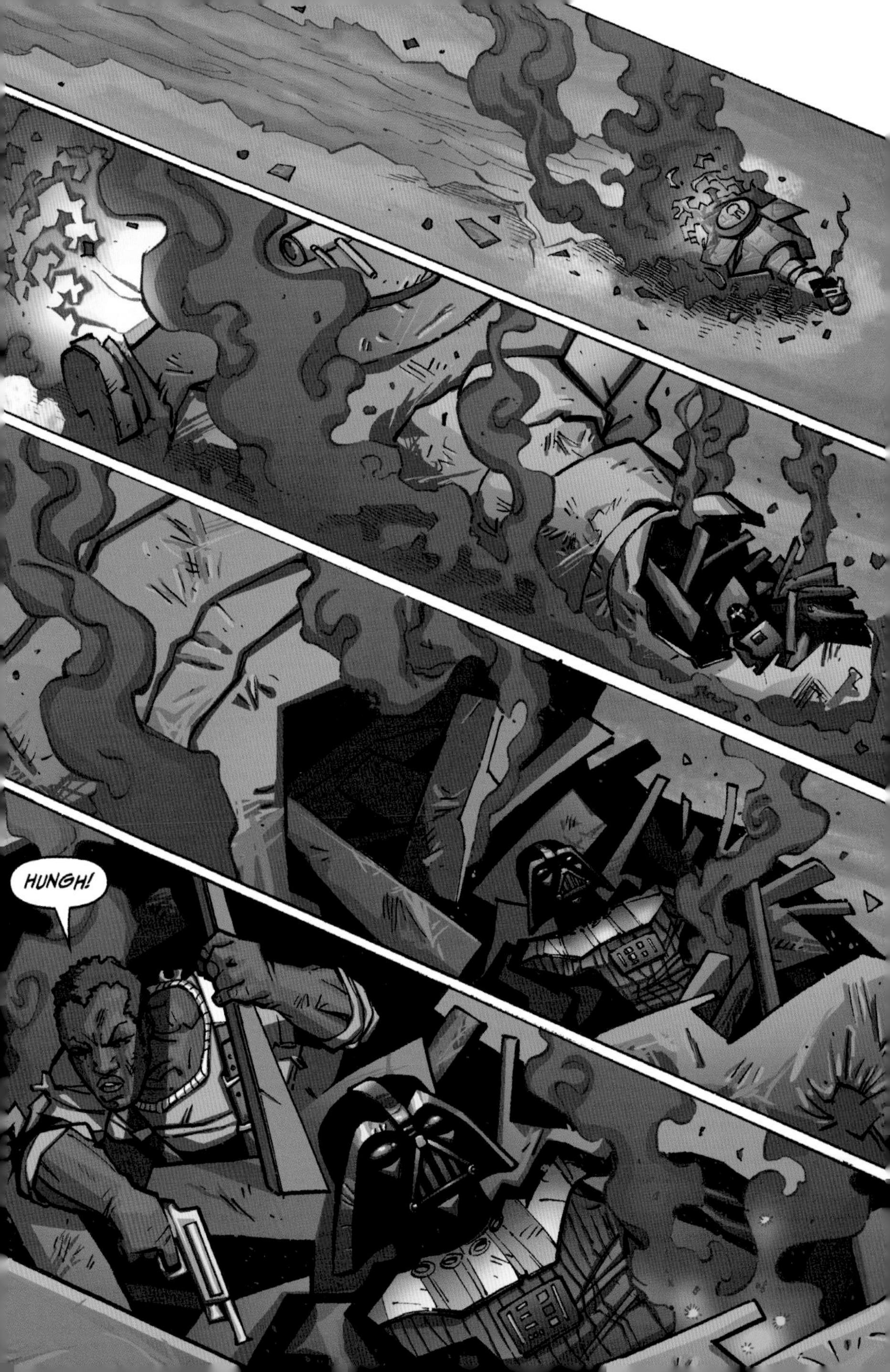
HUNGH!

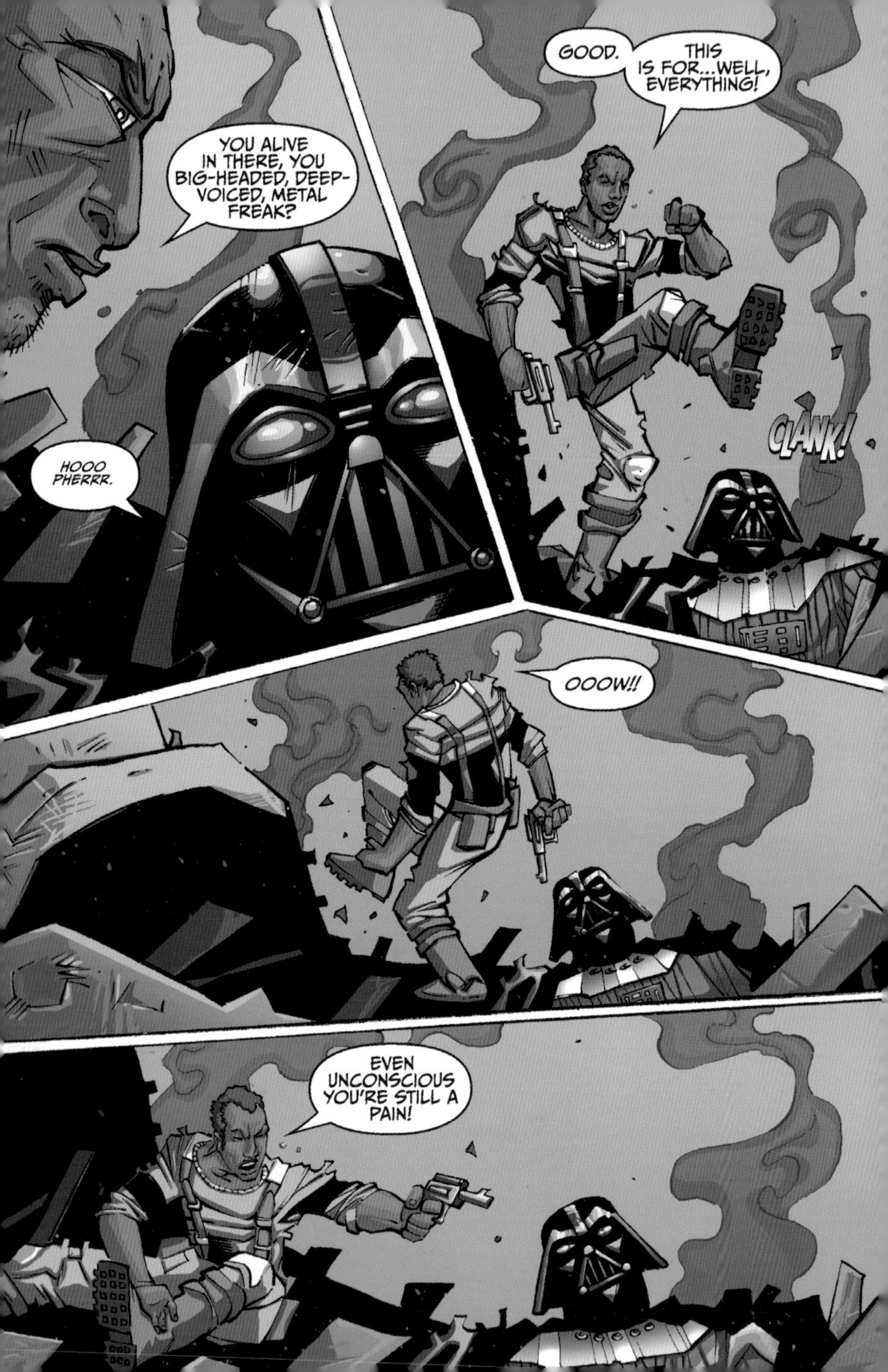

YOU ALIVE IN THERE, YOU BIG-HEADED, DEEP-VOICED, METAL FREAK?
HOOO PHERRR.
GOOD.
THIS IS FOR...WELL, EVERYTHING!
CLANK!
OOOW!!
EVEN UNCONSCIOUS YOU'RE STILL A PAIN!

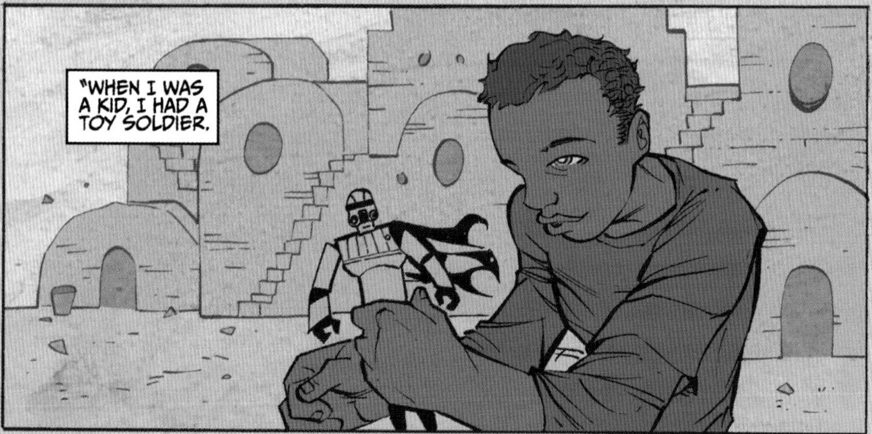
"WHEN I WAS A KID, I HAD A TOY SOLDIER.

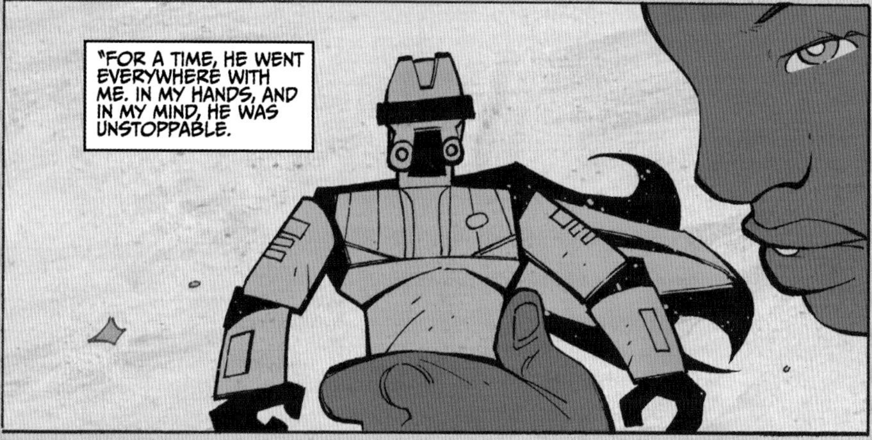
"FOR A TIME, HE WENT EVERYWHERE WITH ME. IN MY HANDS, AND IN MY MIND, HE WAS UNSTOPPABLE.

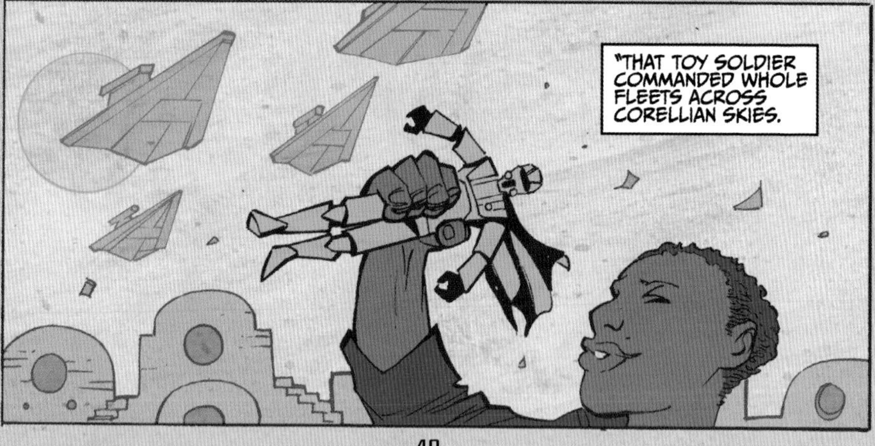
"THAT TOY SOLDIER COMMANDED WHOLE FLEETS ACROSS CORELLIAN SKIES.

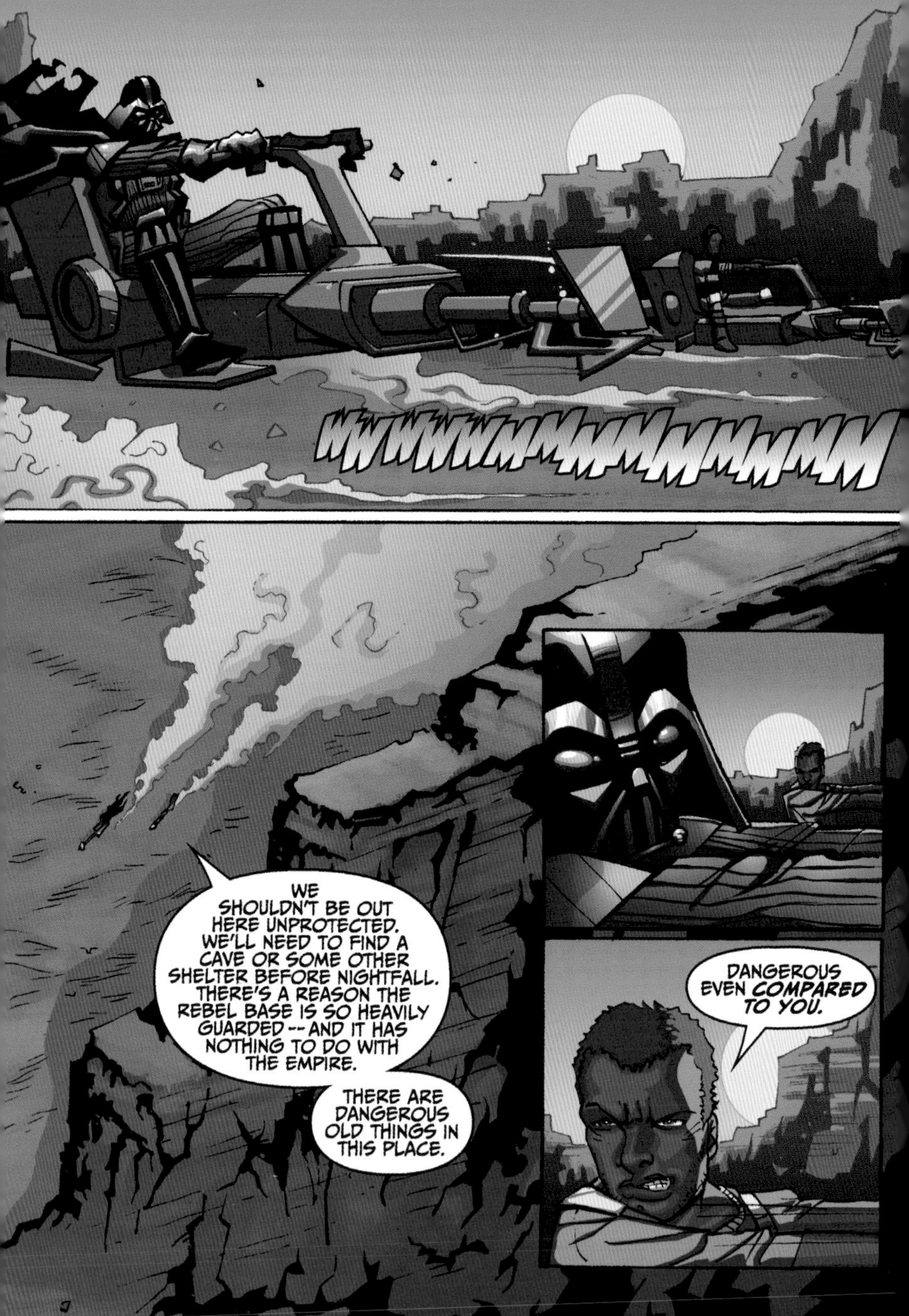
WWWWWMMMMMMMMMMM
WE SHOULDN'T BE OUT HERE UNPROTECTED. WE'LL NEED TO FIND A CAVE OR SOME OTHER SHELTER BEFORE NIGHTFALL. THERE'S A REASON THE REBEL BASE IS SO HEAVILY GUARDED--AND IT HAS NOTHING TO DO WITH THE EMPIRE.
THERE ARE DANGEROUS OLD THINGS IN THIS PLACE.
DANGEROUS EVEN COMPARED TO YOU.

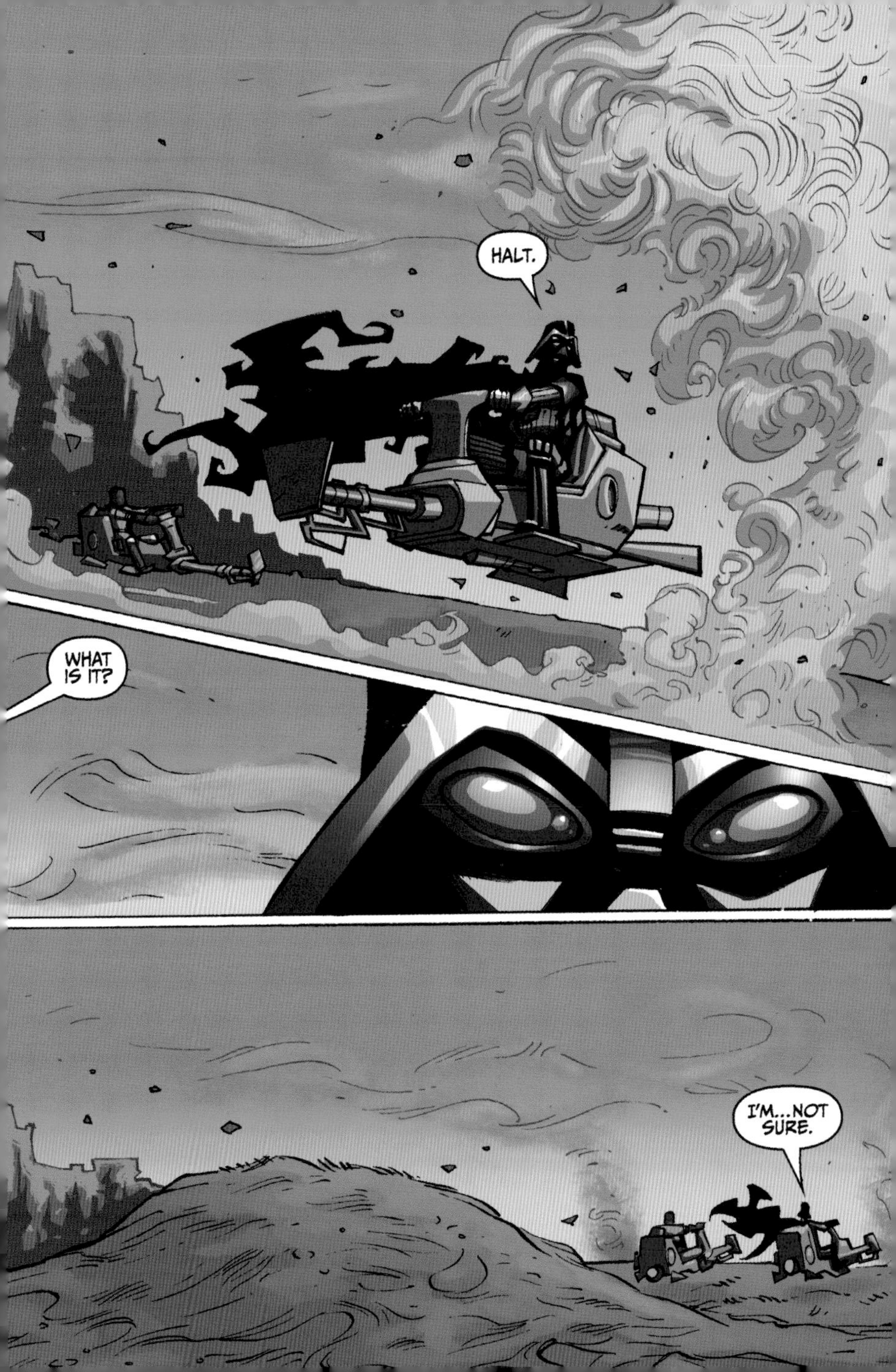
HALT.
WHAT IS IT?
I'M...NOT SURE.

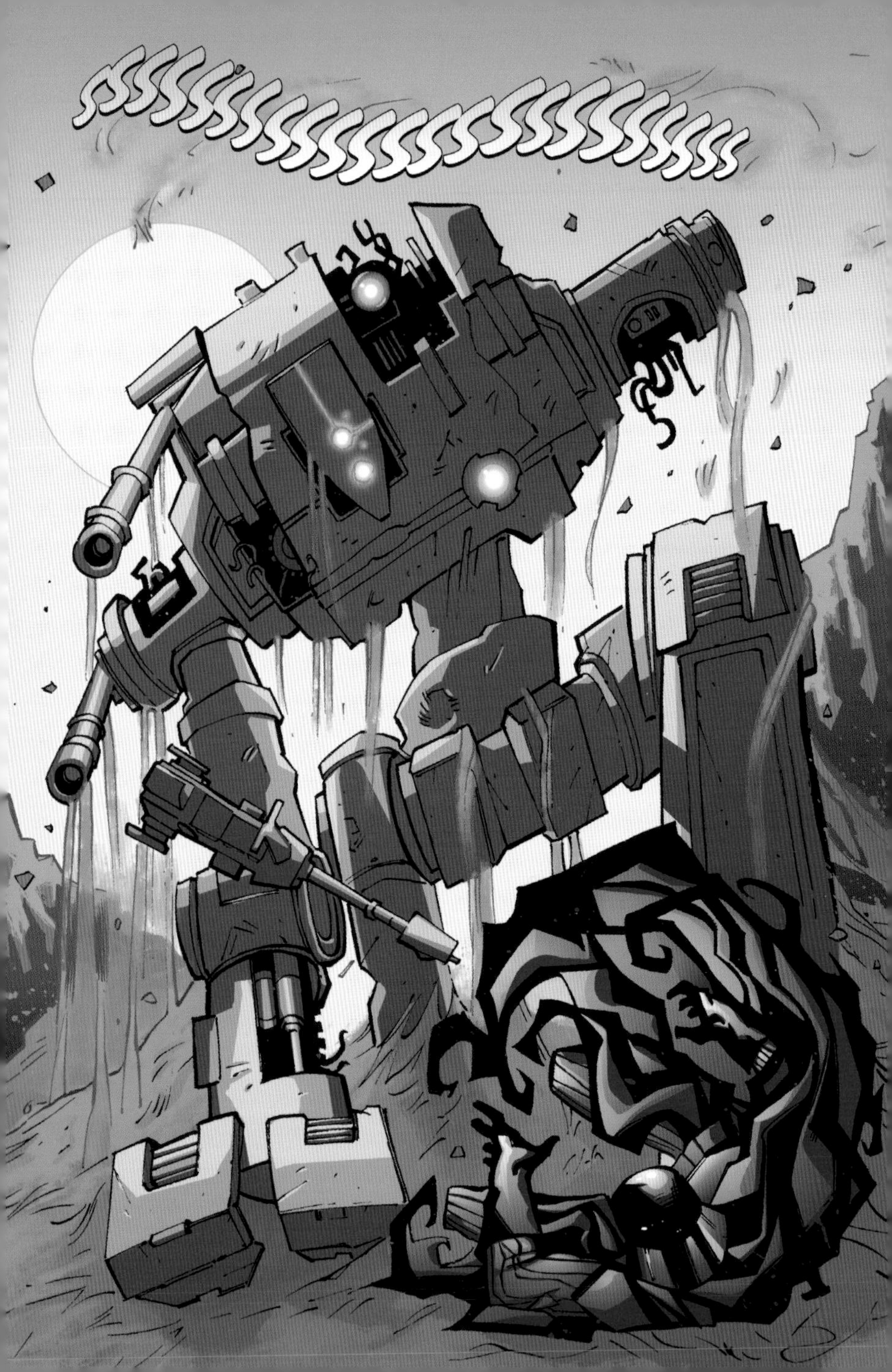
SSSSSSSSSSSSSSSSSSSSSSSS

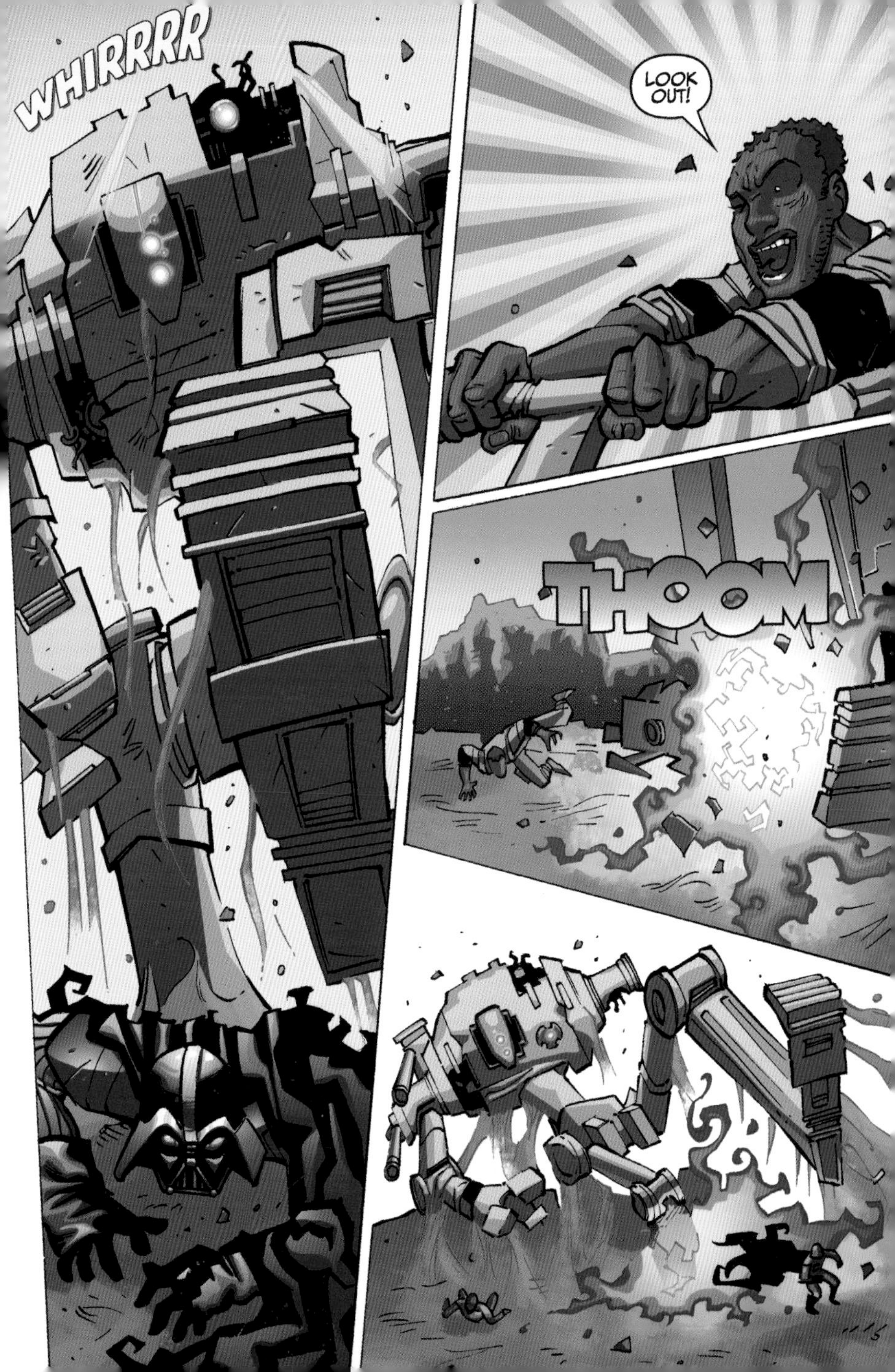
WHIRRRR
LOOK OUT!
THOOM

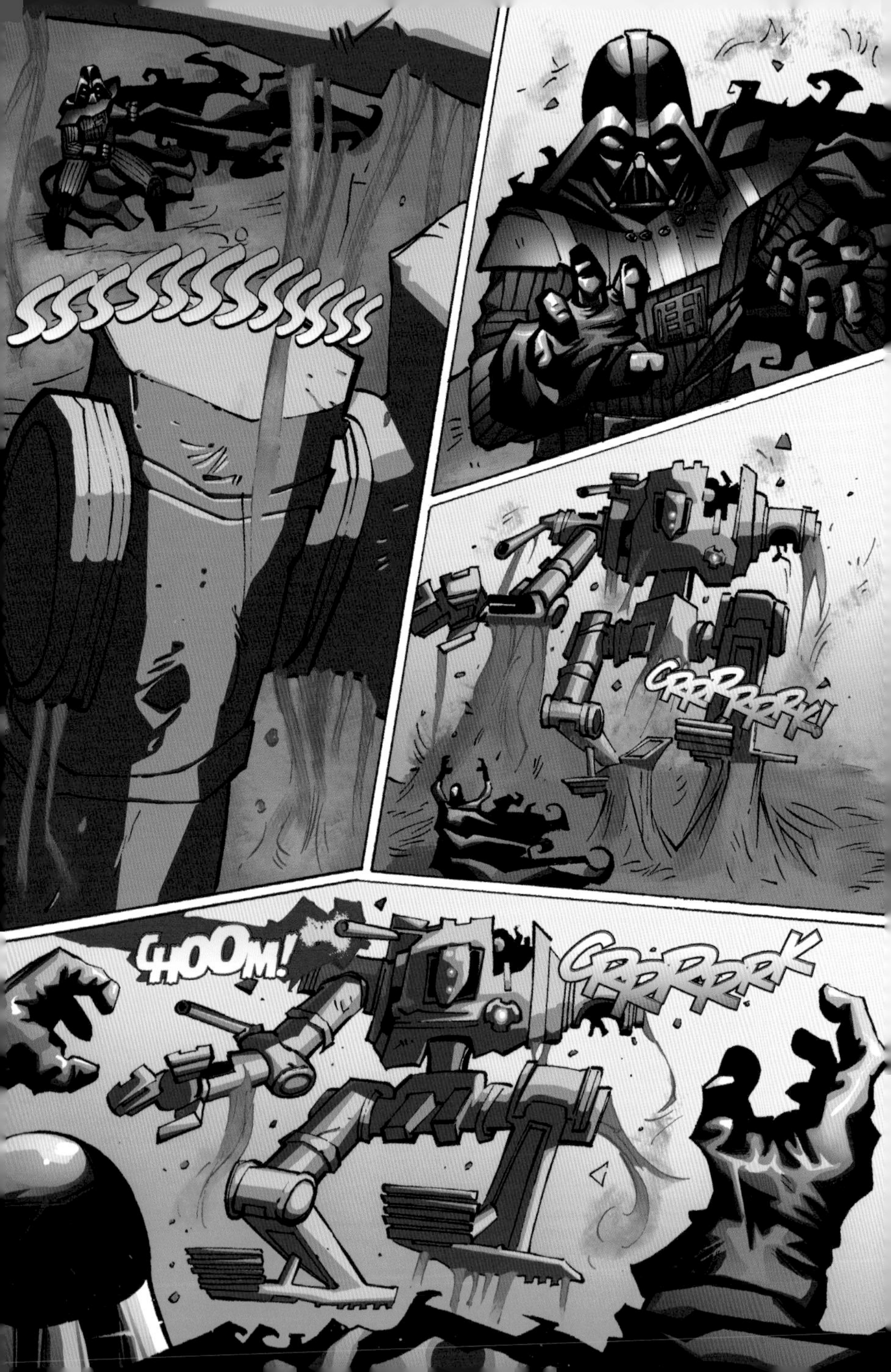
SSSSSSSSSSSSSSS
GRRRRRRK!
CHOOM!
GRRRRRRK

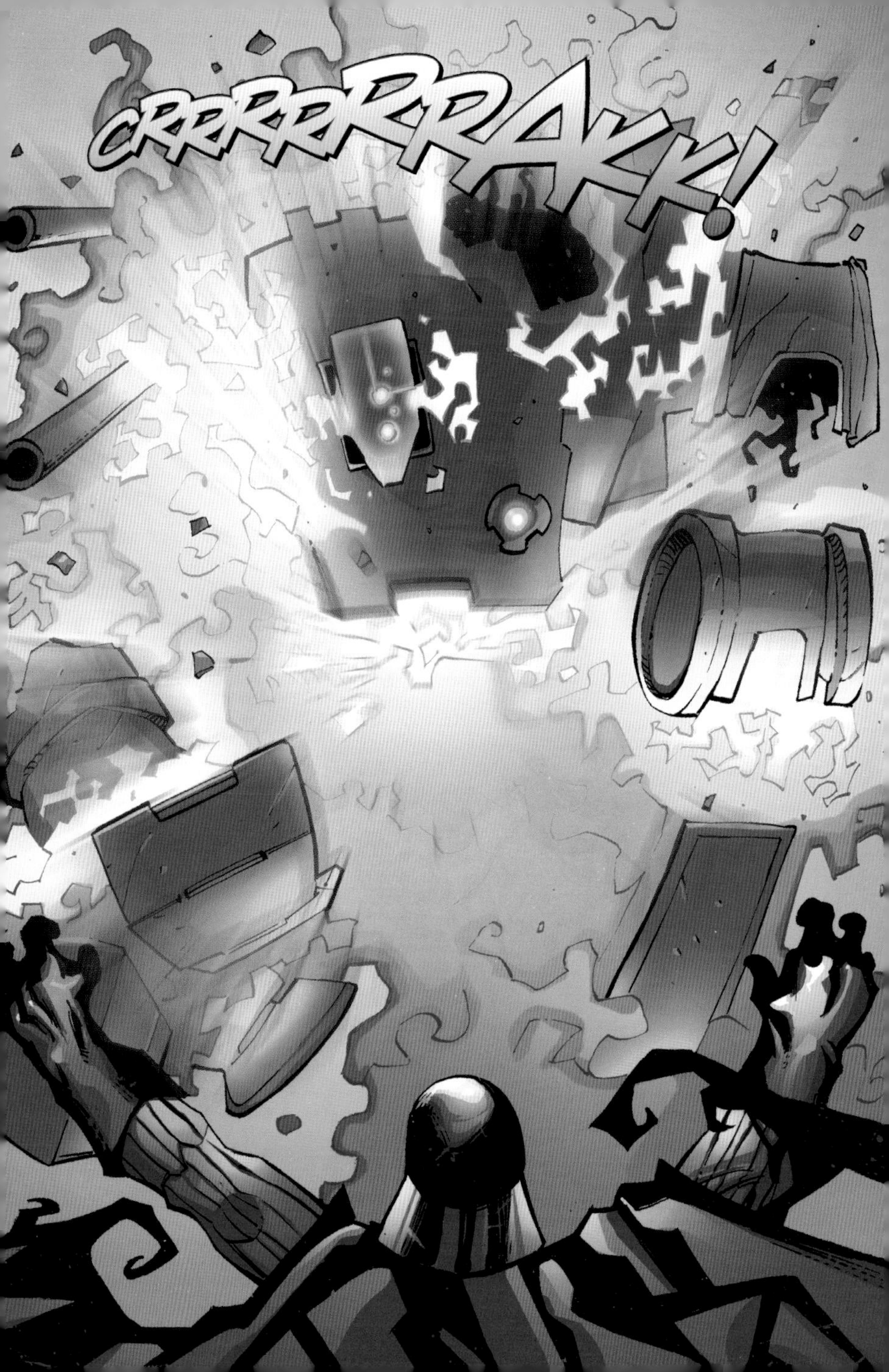
CRRRRRRRAKK!

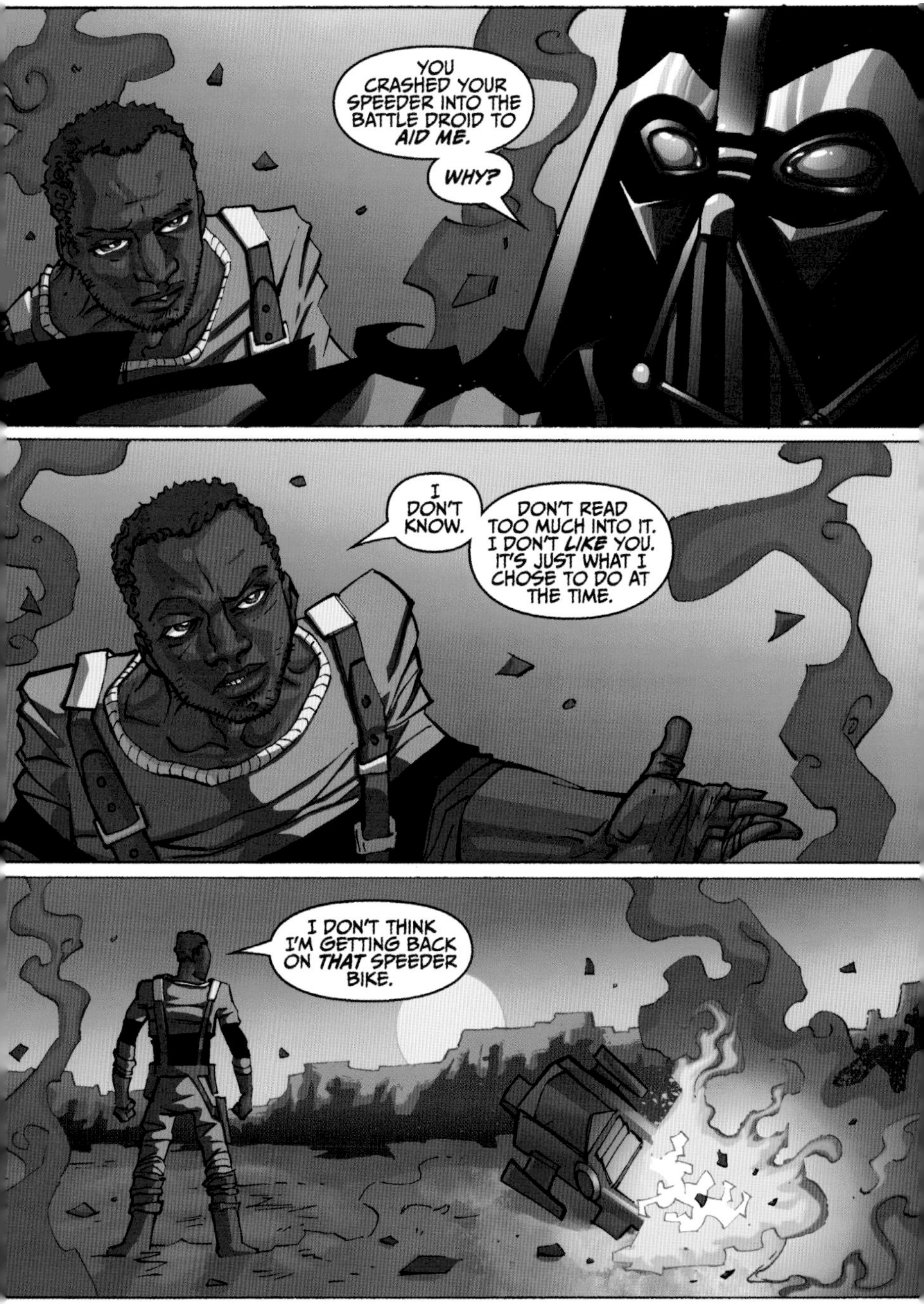
YOU CRASHED YOUR SPEEDER INTO THE BATTLE DROID TO AID ME.
WHY?
I DON'T KNOW.
DON'T READ TOO MUCH INTO IT. I DON'T LIKE YOU. IT'S JUST WHAT I CHOSE TO DO AT THE TIME.
I DON'T THINK I'M GETTING BACK ON THAT SPEEDER BIKE.

"SLEEP..."

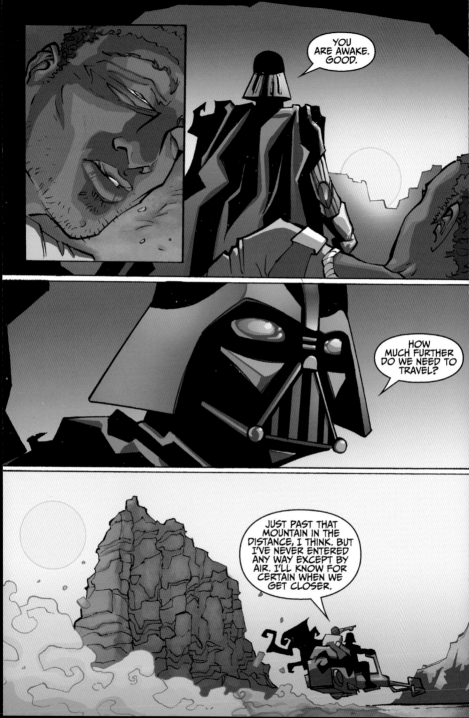

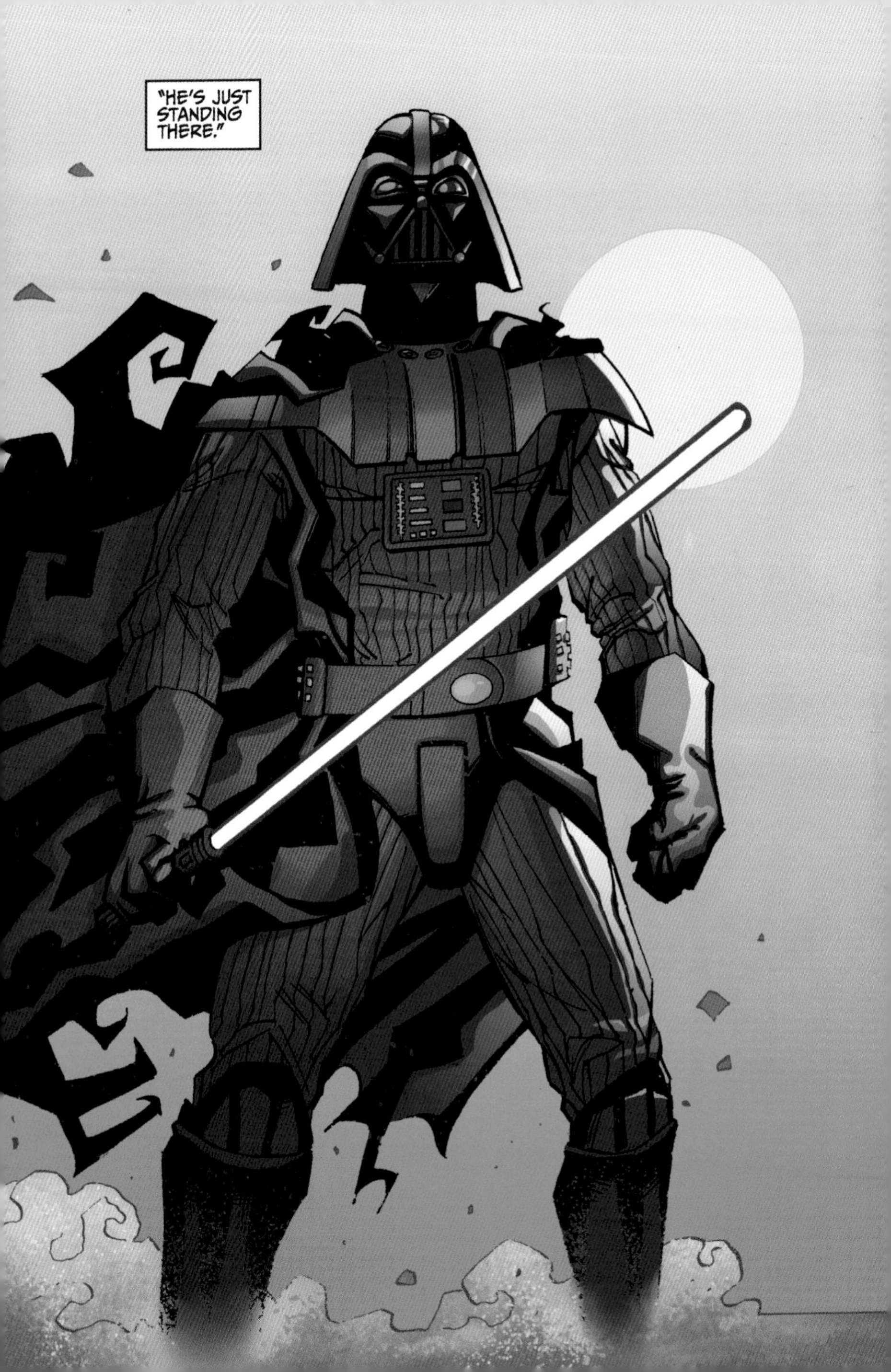
"HE'S JUST STANDING THERE."

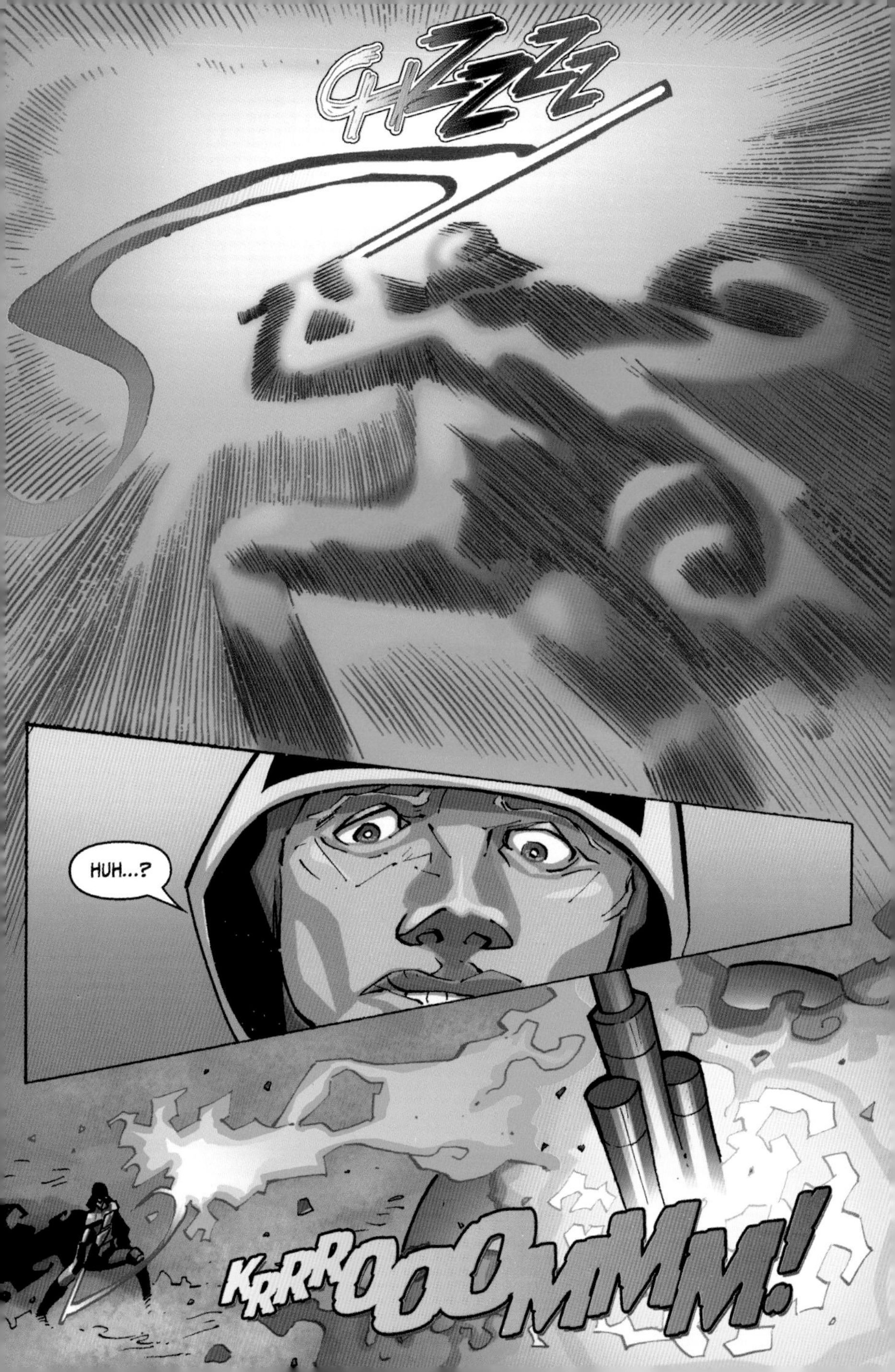
CHZZZZ
HUH...?
KRRROOOOMMMM!

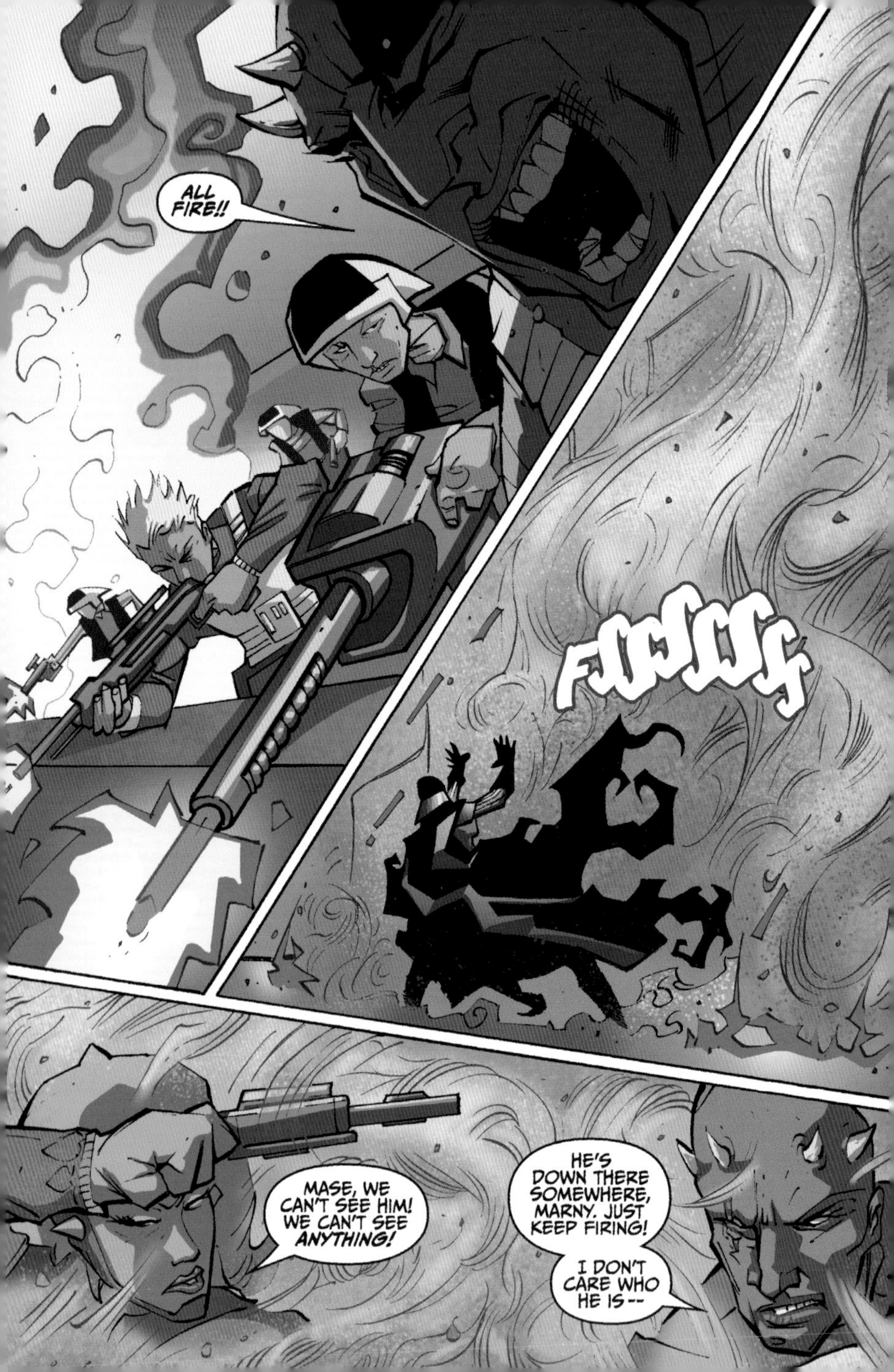
ALL FIRE!!
FOOSSSH
MASE, WE CAN'T SEE HIM! WE CAN'T SEE *ANYTHING*!
HE'S DOWN THERE SOMEWHERE, MARNY. JUST KEEP FIRING!
I DON'T CARE WHO HE IS--

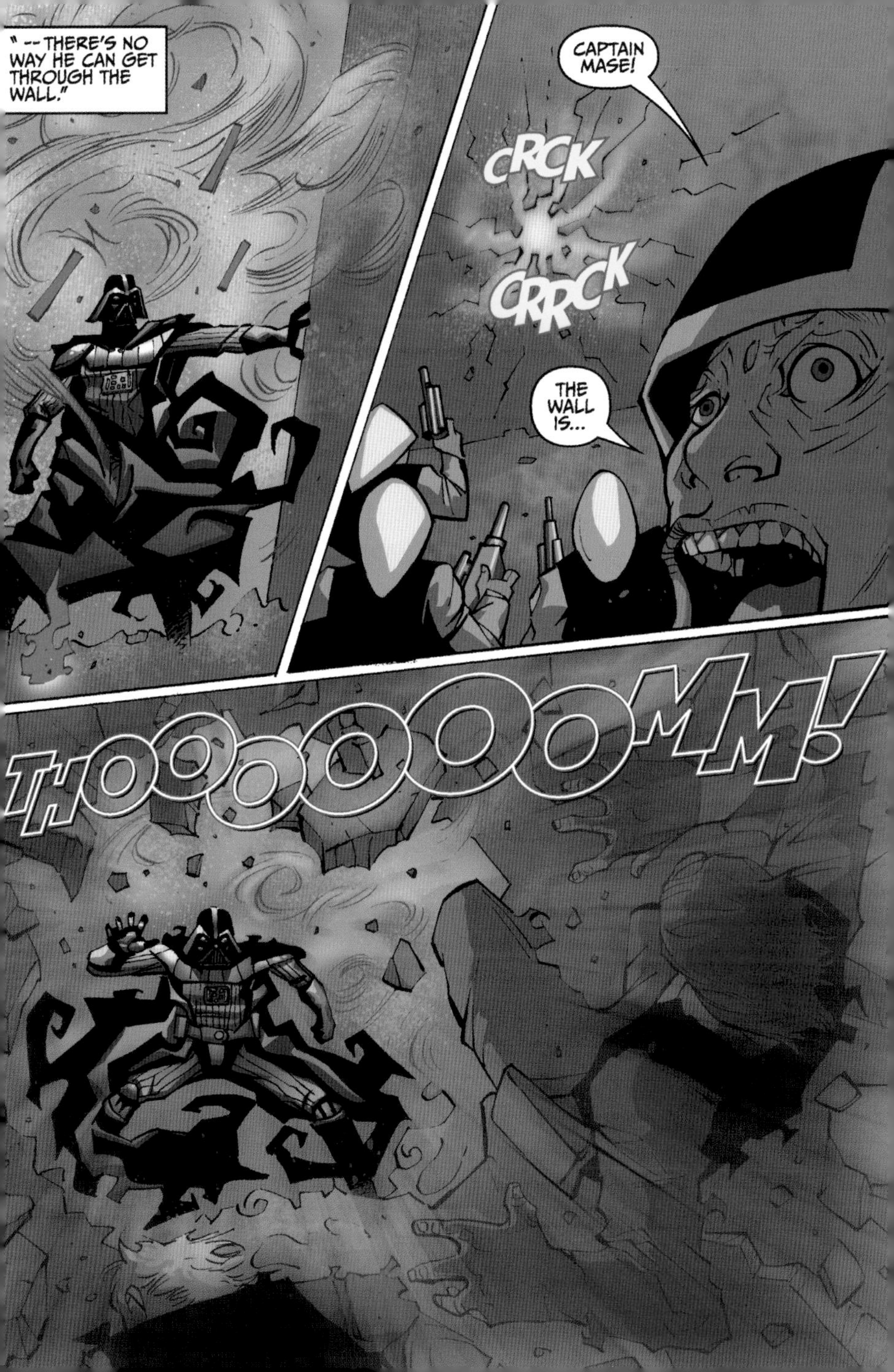
" --THERE'S NO WAY HE CAN GET THROUGH THE WALL."
CAPTAIN MASE!
CRCK
CRRCK
THE WALL IS...
THOOOOOOOMM!

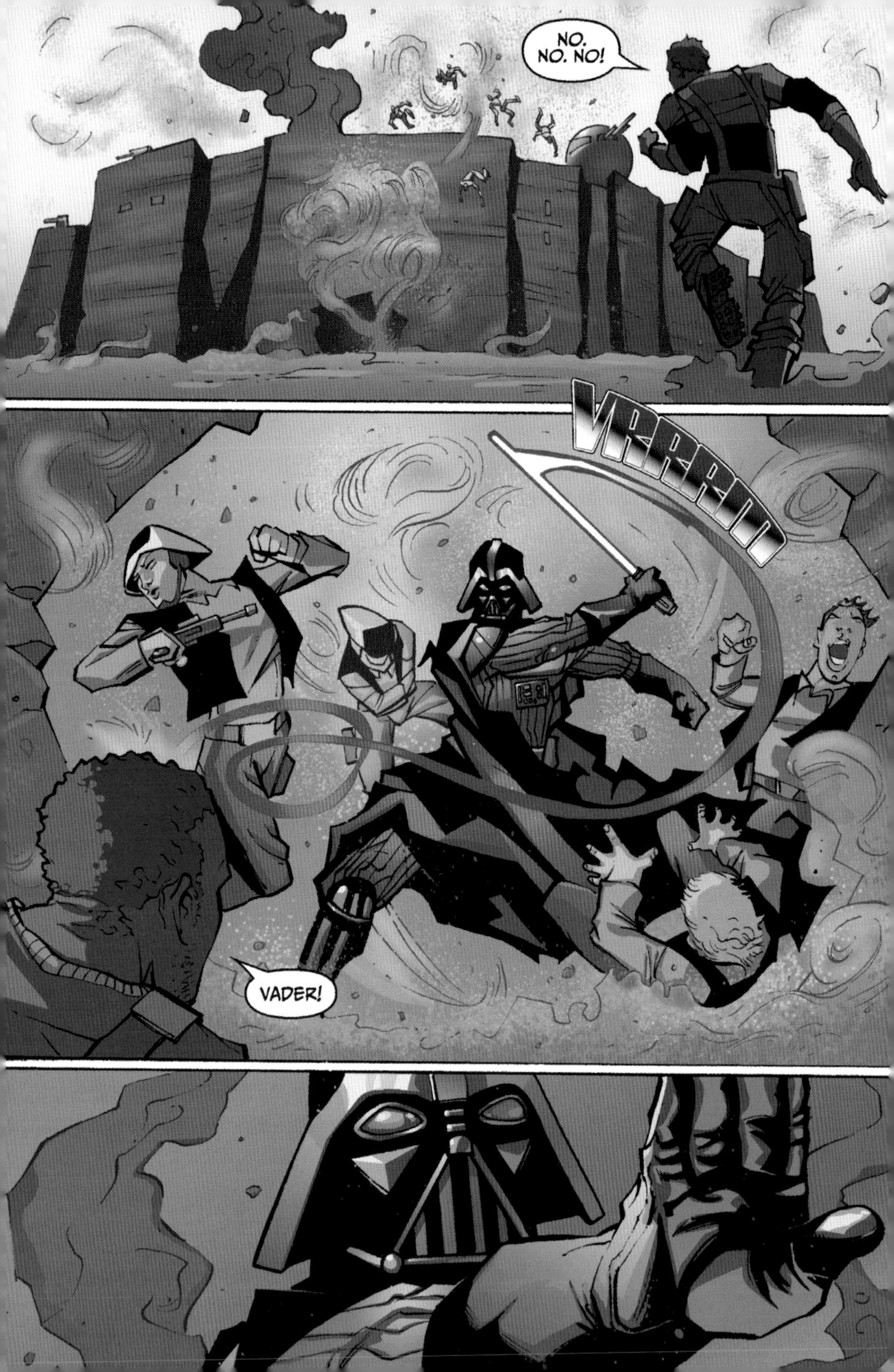
NO. NO. NO!
VRRRMMM
VADER!

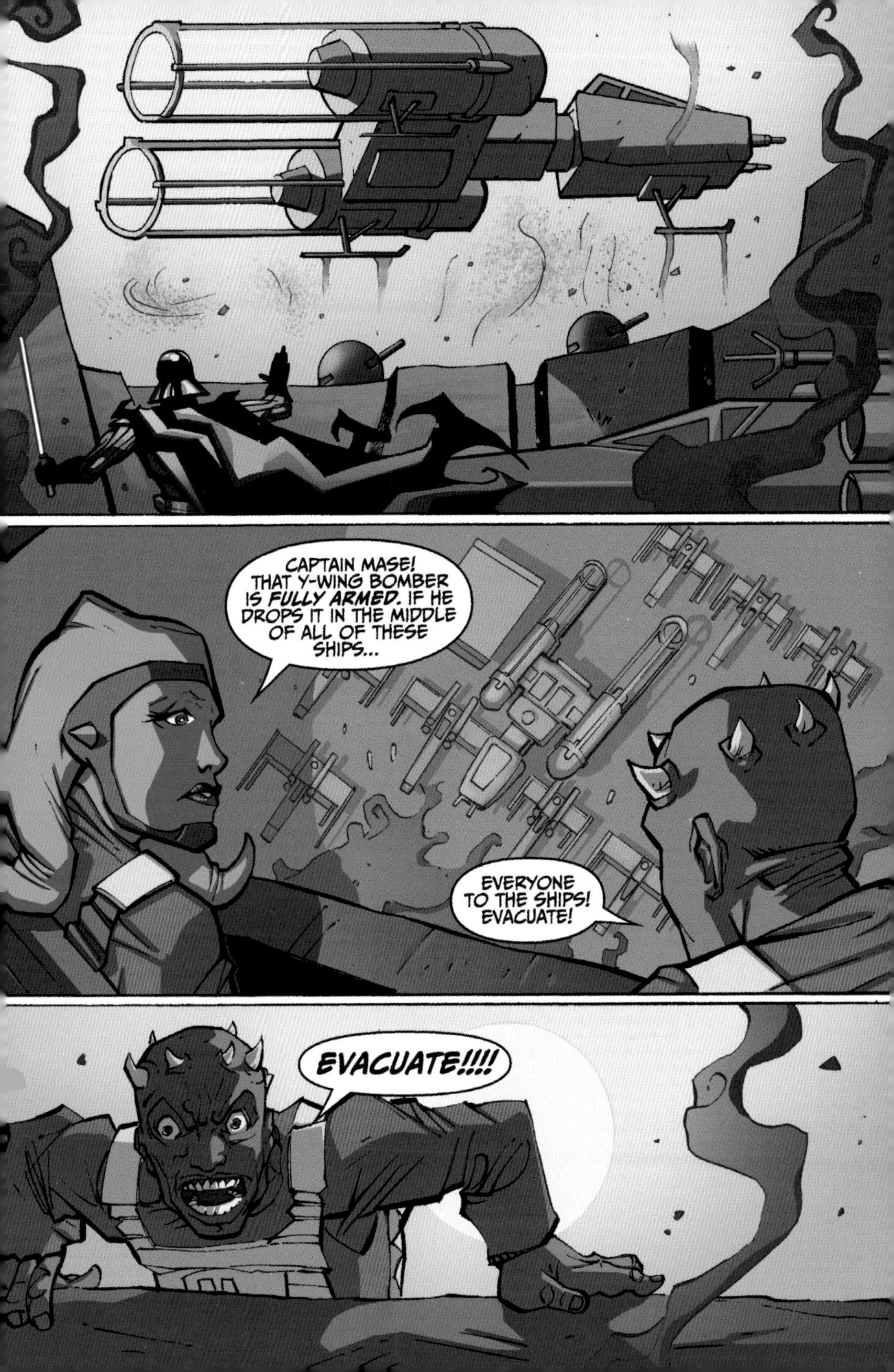
CAPTAIN MASE! THAT Y-WING BOMBER IS FULLY ARMED. IF HE DROPS IT IN THE MIDDLE OF ALL OF THESE SHIPS...
EVERYONE TO THE SHIPS! EVACUATE!
EVACUATE!!!!

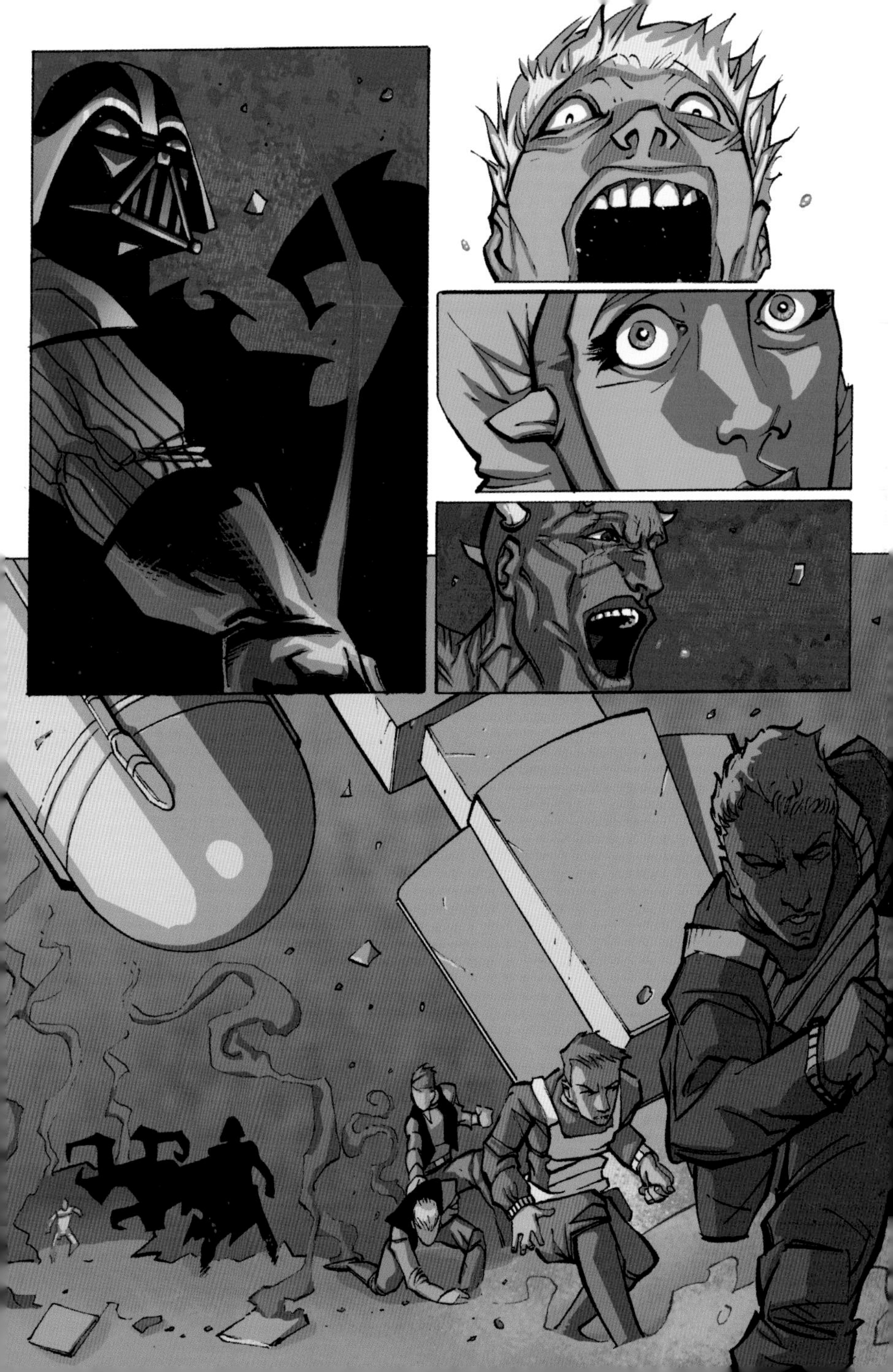

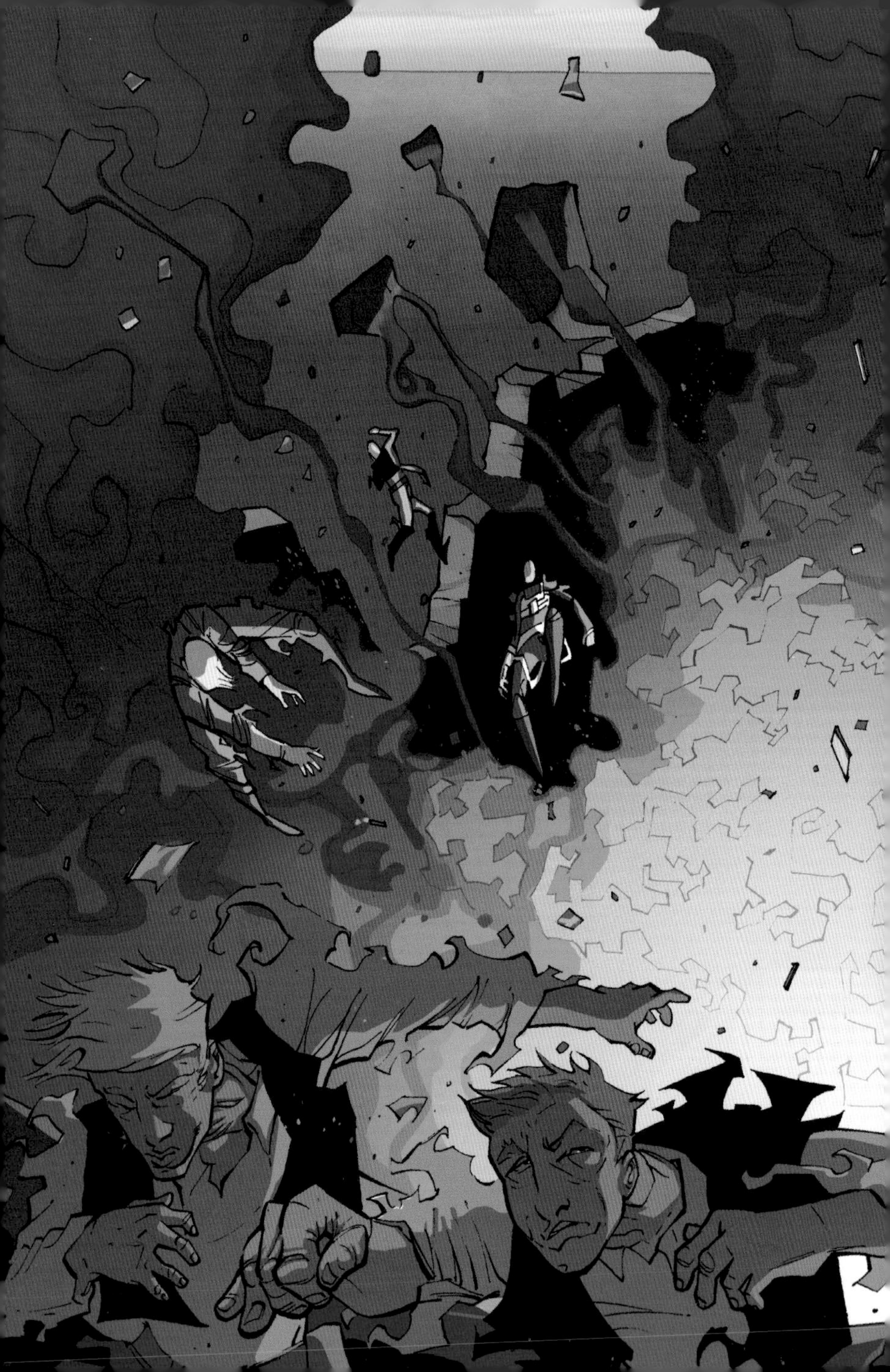

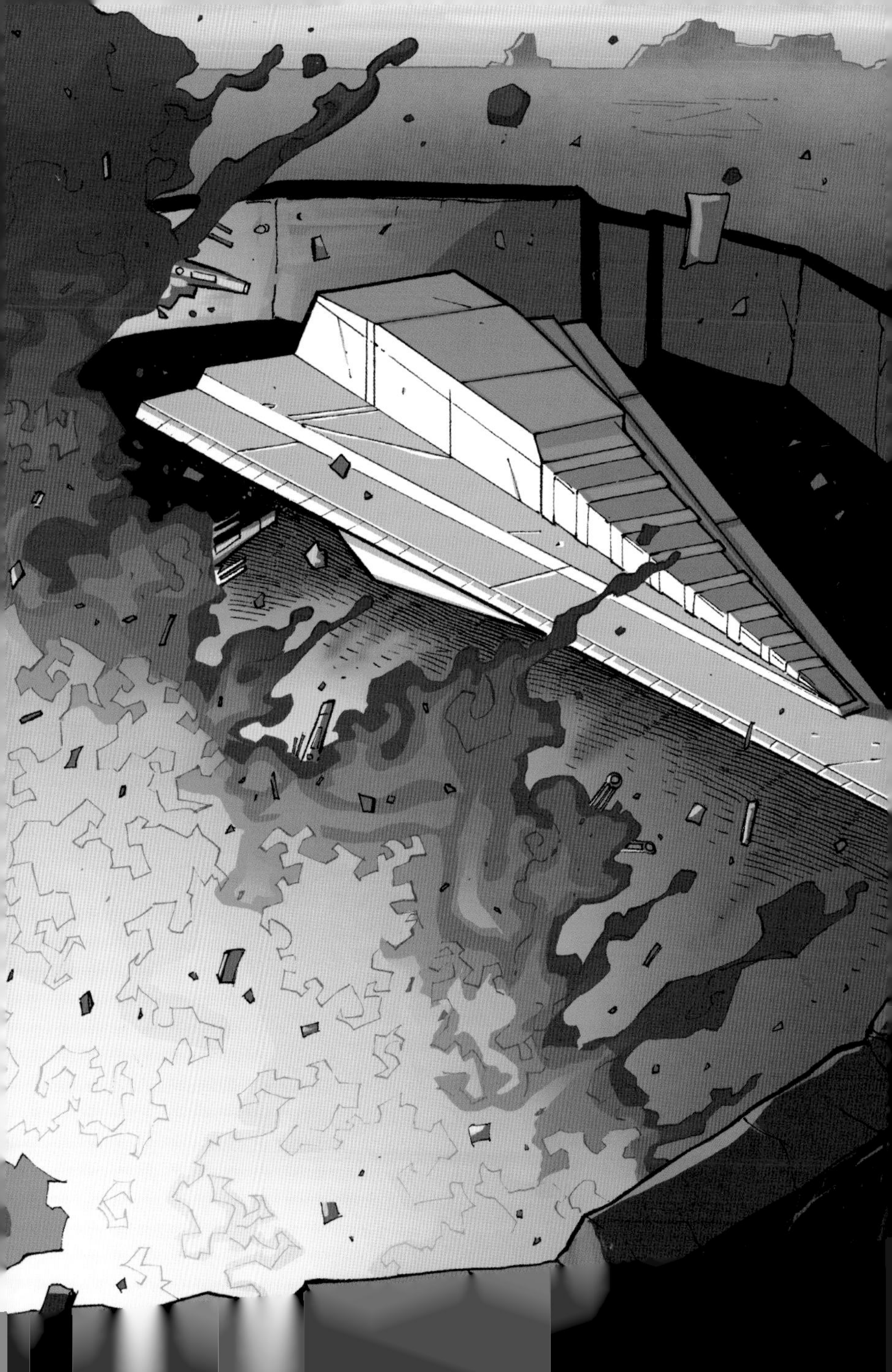

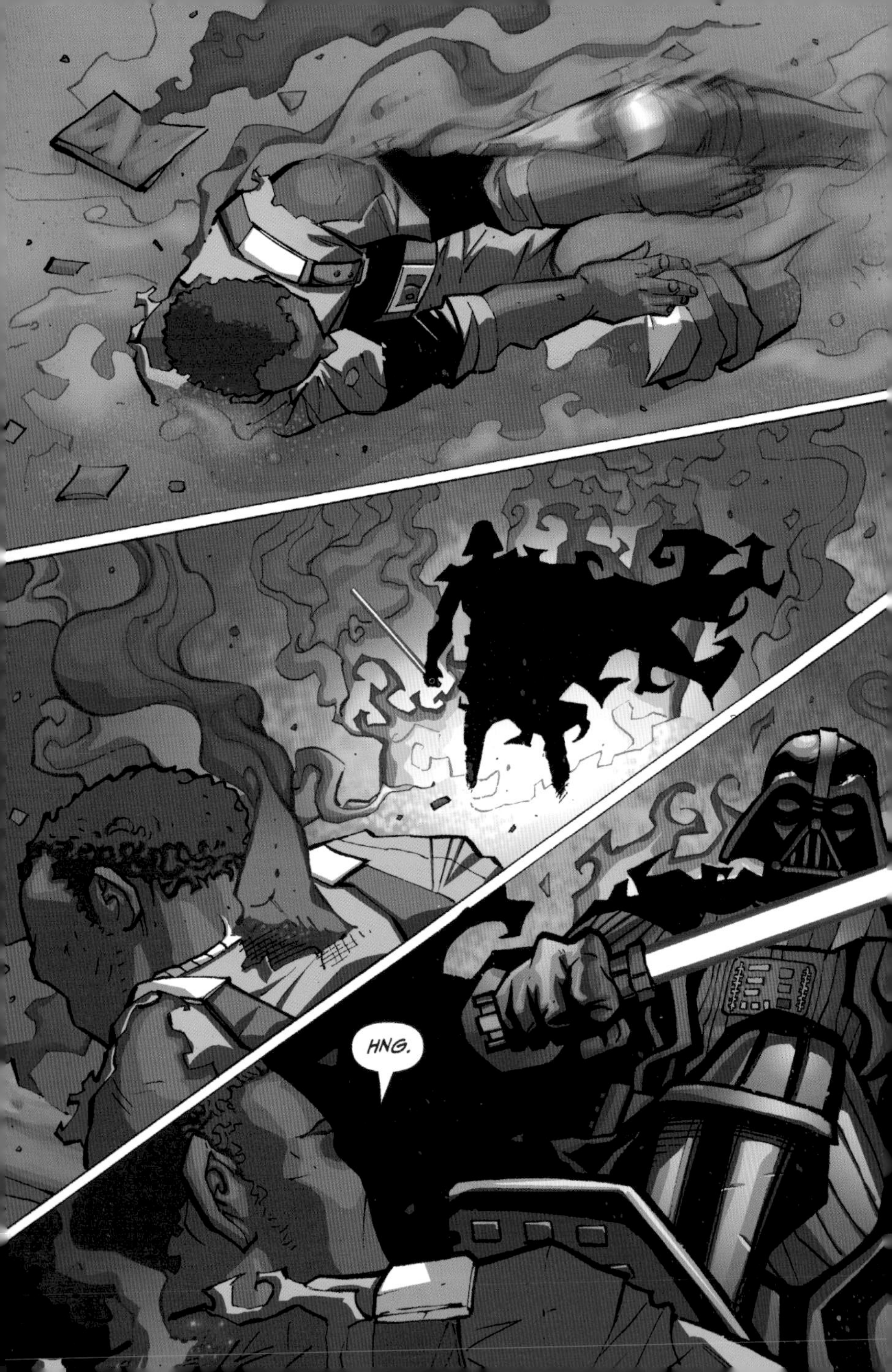
HNG.

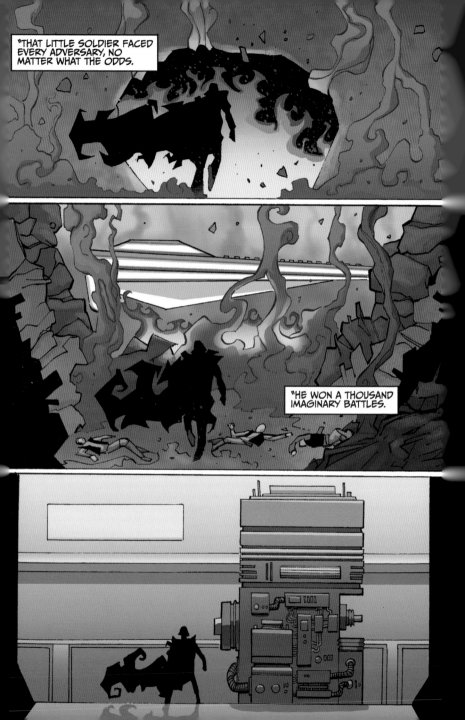

STAR WARS GRAPHIC NOVEL TIMELINE (IN YEARS)

Omnibus: Tales of the Jedi—5,000–3,986 BSW4
Knights of the Old Republic—3,964–3,963 BSW4
Jedi vs. Sith—1,000 BSW4
Omnibus: Rise of the Sith—33 BSW4
Episode I: The Phantom Menace—32 BSW4
Omnibus: Emissaries and Assassins—32 BSW4
Twilight—31 BSW4
Bounty Hunters—31 BSW4
The Hunt for Aurra Sing—30 BSW4
Darkness—30 BSW4
The Stark Hyperspace War—30 BSW4
Rite of Passage—28 BSW4
Jango Fett—27 BSW4
Zam Wesell—27 BSW4
Honor and Duty—24 BSW4
Episode II: Attack of the Clones—22 BSW4
Clone Wars—22–19 BSW4
Clone Wars Adventures—22–19 BSW4
General Grievous—22–19 BSW4
Episode III: Revenge of the Sith—19 BSW4
Dark Times—19 BSW4
Omnibus: Droids—5.5 BSW4
Boba Fett: Enemy of the Empire—3 BSW4
Underworld—1 BSW4
Episode IV: A New Hope—SW4
Classic Star Wars—0–3 ASW4
A Long Time Ago . . . —0–4 ASW4
Empire—0 ASW4
Rebellion—0 ASW4
Boba Fett: Man with a Mission—0 ASW4
Omnibus: Early Victories—0–3 ASW4
Jabba the Hutt: The Art of the Deal—1 ASW4
Episode V: The Empire Strikes Back—3 ASW4
Shadows of the Empire—3.5 ASW4
Episode VI: Return of the Jedi—4 ASW4
Mara Jade: By the Emperor's Hand—4 ASW4
Omnibus: X-Wing Rogue Squadron—4–5 ASW4
Heir to the Empire—9 ASW4
Dark Force Rising—9 ASW4
The Last Command—9 ASW4
Dark Empire—10 ASW4
Boba Fett: Death, Lies, and Treachery—10 ASW4
Crimson Empire—11 ASW4
Jedi Academy: Leviathan—12 ASW4
Union—19 ASW4
Chewbacca—25 ASW4
Legacy—130–137 ASW4

Old Republic Era
25,000 – 1000 years before
Star Wars: A New Hope

Rise of the Empire Era
1000 – 0 years before
Star Wars: A New Hope

Rebellion Era
0 – 5 years after
Star Wars: A New Hope

New Republic Era
5 – 25 years after
Star Wars: A New Hope

New Jedi Order Era
25+ years after
Star Wars: A New Hope

Legacy Era
130+ years after
Star Wars: A New Hope

Infinities
Does not apply to timeline

Sergio Aragonés Stomps Star Wars
Star Wars Tales
Star Wars Infinities
Tag and Bink
Star Wars Visionaries

BSW4 = before *Episode IV: A New Hope*. ASW4 = after *Episode IV: A New Hope*.